Spotlight on Young Children

Cristina Gillanders & Rossella Procopio EDITORS

National Association for the Education of Young Children
Washington, DC

naeyc®

National Association for the
Education of Young Children
1313 L Street NW, Suite 500
Washington, DC 20005-4101
202-232-8777 • 800-424-2460
NAEYC.org

NAEYC Books

Senior Director, Publishing
and Professional Learning
Susan Friedman

Editor in Chief
Kathy Charner

Senior Editor
Holly Bohart

Editor
Rossella Procopio

Senior Creative Design Manager
Henrique J. Siblesz

Senior Creative Design Specialist
Charity Coleman

Publishing Business
Operations Manager
Francine Markowitz

Through its publications
program, the National
Association for the Education
of Young Children (NAEYC)
provides a forum for discussion
of major issues and ideas in the
early childhood field, with the
hope of provoking thought and
promoting professional growth.
The views expressed or implied
in this book are not necessarily
those of the Association.

The following selections were previously published in the specified
issues of *Young Children*: S. Bernheimer and E. Jones, "The Gifts of
the Stranger: Learning from Others' Differences," September 2013;
P. Pilonieta, P.L. Shue, and B.T. Kissel, "Reading Books, Writing Books:
Reading and Writing Come Together in a Dual Language Classroom,"
July 2014; J.K. Adair and A. Barraza, "Voices of Immigrant Parents in
Preschool Settings," September 2014; A.P. Peixoto da Silva, "Supporting
Gay and Lesbian Families in the Early Childhood Classroom," September
2014; I. Alanís, I. Salinas-Gonzalez, and M.G. Arreguín-Anderson,
"Developing Biliteracy with Intentional Support: Using Interactive Word
Walls and Paired Learning," September 2015; L.P. Kuh, D. LeeKeenan,
H. Given, and M.R. Beneke, "Moving Beyond Anti-Bias Activities:
Supporting the Development of Anti-Bias Practices," March 2016;
I.E. Murray and A.J. Alvarez, "Research to Practice: New Research on
Helping Young Children Develop Positive Racial Identities," November
2016; T. DosRemedios, "Building a More Inclusive Sandbox: Inviting
New Collaborators to Support Children, Families, and Early Learning,"
November 2016; B.T. Bowman, J.P. Comer, and D.J. Johns, "Addressing
the African American Achievement Gap: Three Leading Educators
Issue a Call to Action," May 2018; K. Cole and D. Verwayne, "Becoming
Upended: Teaching and Learning About Race and Racism with Young
Children and Their Families," May 2018; and T.C. Howard, "Capitalizing
on Culture: Engaging Young Learners in Diverse Classrooms," May 2018.

The following selection was previously published in the specified issue
of *Teaching Young Children*: N. Jaboneta, with D. Curtis, "Challenging
Gender Stereotypes," February/March 2018.

The following is excerpted from *Ethics and the Early Childhood
Educator: Using the NAEYC Code*, Third Edition (NAEYC, 2018): S.
Feeney and N.K. Freeman, "'Don't Let My Son Dress Up as a Girl!'"

Permissions

NAEYC accepts requests for limited use of our copyrighted material.
For permission to reprint, adapt, translate, or otherwise reuse and
repurpose content from this publication, review our guidelines at
NAEYC.org/resources/permissions.

Portions of "Addressing the African American Achievement Gap: Three
Leading Educators Issue a Call to Action," by Barbara T. Bowman,
James P. Comer, and David J. Johns on pages 45–56, are adapted, with
the authors' permission, from *Early Learning: A Report for the White
House Initiative on Educational Excellence for African Americans*. This
unpublished report was developed in 2015 while David Johns was
the executive director of the White House Initiative on Educational
Excellence for African Americans during the Obama administration.

Cover Photo Credits

Library of Congress Control Number: 2018911345

ISBN: 978-1-938113-41-3

Item 2843

Contents

Introduction

Cristina Gillanders

> All children have the right to equitable learning opportunities that help them achieve their full potential as engaged learners and valued members of society. Early childhood educators have a professional obligation to advance equity and diversity.
>
> —NAEYC's forthcoming position statement on equity and diversity

Every young child brings to the classroom a wealth of unique and complex knowledge, skills, and experiences. As children interact with their families and communities in everyday contexts, they begin to understand how the world works and how to respond to the expectations of their families and their communities. As they raise children, adults create these contexts by following traditions and routines they learned from previous generations and considering their children's abilities and characteristics. They also create learning opportunities for children in response to what they perceive to be the expectations of the contexts of their community. Consequently, children's learning and development follow culture-specific pathways and can only be fully understood and effectively supported by taking into consideration the cultural beliefs and practices of their communities (Rogoff 2003; Rogoff, Dahl, & Callanan 2018).

NAEYC's Forthcoming Position Statement on Equity & Diversity

By NAEYC

Anti-bias education has long guided NAEYC's work to promote high-quality early learning for all young children. With the forthcoming release of its position statement on equity and diversity, NAEYC is highlighting its commitment to leading early childhood educators in recognizing, overcoming, and eliminating the personal biases and structural and institutional inequities that prevent children from marginalized groups from experiencing the same learning opportunities and advantages as their peers.

This position statement as well as some of the articles in this volume call attention to the emerging research base on implicit bias, which reveals that teachers' implicit bias can impact their perceptions of children's learning and development. For example, research indicates that teachers often view the play of children of color—particularly African American boys—differently than that of other children. Self-reflection is one way teachers can develop an awareness of, recognize, and mediate bias and barriers in all areas of teaching to ensure that all children experience needed cognitive, social, and linguistic advantages that prepare them for future success in school. Each of the articles in this volume includes a set of reflection questions to guide educators in their journey. In fact, the first two articles in this volume (see "The Gifts of the Stranger: Learning from Others' Differences" on page 5 and "Moving Beyond Anti-Bias Activities: Supporting the Development of Anti-Bias Practices" on page 17) focus on self-reflection themselves, an important first step in the journey of supporting the development and learning of all children.

There is far more to be explored regarding this issue than any one resource can achieve. Just as the equity and diversity position statement acts as a starting point with broad-stroke guidance that individual educators must build upon, this volume of *Spotlight on Young Children* has been compiled within the limitations of a publication with finite space. This book is only the beginning of resources from NAEYC centered on equity and diversity.

Often, schools and educators do not value the learning experiences that emerge from children's everyday contexts if those experiences are not compatible with school culture and the expectations schools have for children. As such, children from historically underserved populations are often considered to have a deficit and, consequently, are thought to be at risk for not succeeding in school. This notion of *deficit* comes both from a lack of recognition of the value of children's background knowledge and administrators' and teachers' limited understanding of how the cultural knowledge learned at home and in the community relates to the knowledge and skills learned in school. These deficit views can deprive children of color of learning experiences in school reserved for those who come from more privileged or advantaged populations.

Given this, how do early childhood teachers create experiences that build on what children already know and understand? The first step is to identify children's experiences or background knowledge so that they can effectively bridge it to what is necessary to learn in school (see "Capitalizing on Culture: Engaging Young Learners in Diverse Classrooms" on page 31). A strong sense of curiosity about children's lives and desire to support their well-being will motivate teachers to learn about children and their families through observations and conversations about their culture, traditions, practices, and beliefs (see "Voices of Immigrant Families in Early Childhood Settings" on page 57).

Teachers must also examine their own racial, socioeconomic, cultural, linguistic, able-bodied, and gender privilege, recognizing and reflecting on how their personal identity and implicit or explicit biases inform a deficit approach to differences. Only then can they approach children and their families from a stance of respect and curiosity (see "Supporting Gay and Lesbian Families in the Early Childhood Classroom" on page 97). This attitude allows teachers to establish positive relationships with families and to create learning environments that support and value children's racial, ethnic, and gender identities; abilities; and funds of knowledge (Moll et al. 1992). At the same time, it enables children to feel confident about who they and their families are and the unique strengths—the knowledge, skills, and experiences—that they bring to the classroom.

The articles in this volume provide examples that illustrate how teachers can build on families' cultural beliefs and practices to create culturally sustaining pedagogies. Culturally sustaining pedagogy goes beyond merely being responsive to the children's and families' experiences—it promotes and sustains children's skills and knowledge learned in their community contexts *and* gives children opportunities to acquire the knowledge and skills needed to succeed in school (Paris 2012). When children learn to value themselves as well as others, they feel safe to explore issues of social justice that are close to them (see "Becoming Upended: Teaching and Learning About Race and Racism with Young Children and Their Families" on page 85). Ultimately, as educators we hope that the children we teach will one day become agents of social change for a better world.

Cristina Gillanders is associate professor of early childhood education in the School of Education and Human Development at University of Colorado Denver. Her research interests include bilingual children's learning and development and home–school partnerships.

———————————

Susan Bernheimer and **Elizabeth Jones** begin this collection of articles with an eye toward self-reflection in "The Gifts of the Stranger: Learning from Others' Differences." Through the lens of their experiences in adult learning environments, the authors explore how recognizing diverse life experiences and circumstances is a critical part of creating equitable learning opportunities.

"Moving Beyond Anti-Bias Activities: Supporting the Development of Anti-Bias Practices" asks educators to consider the ways in which anti-bias education can support proactive, responsive curriculum development and interactions with children. **Lisa P. Kuh**, **Debbie LeeKeenan**, **Heidi Given**, and **Margaret R. Beneke** share a framework developed and used by the educators in their program to hold themselves accountable for anti-bias work and apply this framework to real examples from their classrooms.

Our changing ethnic, racial, and cultural landscape is most evident in the nation's schools. In his article, "Capitalizing on Culture: Engaging Young Learners in Diverse Classrooms," **Tyrone C. Howard** underscores why it is imperative that early childhood educators acquire the cultural awareness and essential proficiencies that enable them to effectively teach and foster learning across cultural and racial differences.

In today's climate, it is more urgent than ever to redress the imbalance of resources and opportunities among diverse groups, and the first step is to understand past and present challenges to design more effective early childhood programs. "Addressing the African American Achievement Gap: Three Leading Educators Issue a Call to Action," by **Barbara T. Bowman**, **James P. Comer**, and **David J. Johns**, discusses the effects of centuries of prejudice, discrimination, and other factors that are at the heart of the achievement gap that exists between African Americans and White Americans.

Immigrant families with young children in early education programs have their own ideas about teaching, learning, and relationships, but when stripped down to their core, there are many commonalities with best practices. **Jennifer Keys Adair** and **Alejandra Barraza** review seven suggestions offered by diverse groups of immigrant families from across the United States in their article, "Voices of Immigrant Families in Early Childhood Settings."

In "Challenging Gender Stereotypes: A Teacher's Reflections on Counteracting Gender Biases," **Nadia Jaboneta**, with **Deb Curtis**, recounts an experience in her classroom that brought to the forefront how social constructs influence children's perception of gender roles very early. She reflects on what she—and all teachers—can do in her daily interactions and practices with children to intentionally counteract gender biases.

Because reading and writing are interconnected processes, considering both when addressing and assessing children's literacy skills is critical, especially when children are learning more than one language. In "Reading Books, Writing Books: Reading and Writing Come Together in a Dual Language Classroom," **Paola Pilonieta**, **Pamela L. Shue**, and **Brian T. Kissel** focus on three children to show how teaching and observing reading and writing together in a bilingual classroom allows for more accurate profiles of children's reading and writing abilities.

"Becoming Upended: Teaching and Learning About Race and Racism with Young Children and Their Families" is a collaboration between **Kirsten Cole**, a community college professor and public school parent, and **Diandra Verwayne**, a kindergarten teacher working in Brooklyn, New York. The article documents how Diandra worked with families as they responded to her curriculum addressing issues of race and racism and offers strategies for approaching these complicated but critical conversations.

Children who come from families with nontraditional structures are another diverse population for which educators must strive to create safe spaces. "Supporting Gay and Lesbian Families in the Early Childhood Classroom," by **Anna Paula Peixoto da Silva**, provides practical strategies that teachers can implement to welcome, include, and support gay and lesbian families.

In "Developing Biliteracy with Intentional Support: Using Interactive Word Walls and Paired Learning," **Iliana Alanís**, **Irasema Salinas-Gonzalez**, and **María G. Arreguín-Anderson** discuss how teachers can create opportunities for young children to hear and use language in meaningful settings—critical for all children but most particularly dual language learners—by integrating partner-based learning and interactive word walls in the classroom.

Stephanie Feeney and **Nancy K. Freeman** describe a situation faced by a teacher when a father objects to his son wearing a pink princess costume in "'Don't Let My Son Dress Up as a Girl!': An Ethical Dilemma." In their article, they describe how the teacher uses the NAEYC Code of Ethical Conduct to analyze and resolve the situation. This, and similar cases, challenge educators to think carefully about children's conceptions of gender.

"Research to Practice: New Research on Helping Young Children Develop Positive Racial Identities" recognizes that race remains central to educational inequity and highlights the importance of supporting children's development of a positive racial identity. Authors **Ira E. Murray** and **Adam J. Alvarez** review three questions that every early childhood educator should consider as well as offer recommendations for advancing educational equity.

Titus DosRemedios concludes this collection with a call to action for educators and experts across other fields to collaborate and advocate for the resources needed to provide all children with access to high-quality learning opportunities in his article, "Building a More Inclusive Sandbox: Inviting New Collaborators to Support Children, Families, and Early Learning."

References

Moll, L.C., C. Amanti, D. Neff, & N. Gonzalez. 1992. "Funds of Knowledge for Teaching: Using a Qualitative Approach to Connect Homes and Classrooms." *Theory Into Practice* 31 (2): 132–41.

Paris, D. 2012. "Culturally Sustaining Pedagogy: A Needed Change in Stance, Terminology, and Practice." *Educational Researcher* 41 (3): 93–97.

Rogoff, B. 2003. *The Cultural Nature of Human Development*. New York: Oxford University Press.

Rogoff, B., A. Dahl, & M. Callanan. 2018. "The Importance of Understanding Children's Lived Experience." *Developmental Review* 50 (Part A): 5–15.

The Gifts of the Stranger
Learning from Others' Differences

Susan Bernheimer and Elizabeth Jones

The United States is experiencing an unprecedented rate of change, given the increasing ethnic diversity of our population, the growing number of single-parent families, the increasing number of immigrants and refugees, and the fact that most mothers work outside the home (Laughlin 2013). Some of these changes mean that families place their trust in strangers—that is, early childhood professionals—instead of relatives or neighbors to care for their children.

In 2016, 65.3 percent of mothers with children younger than 6 were in the labor force, and 63.1 percent of mothers with children younger than 3 were working outside the home (BLS 2017). Nearly 15 million children younger than 6 are in some type of child care setting (Child Care Aware of America 2018). Early childhood programs are creating a new kind of community for families, one that can bridge the gap between their private and public lives.

Professional education provides student teachers with basic teaching knowledge, but developing the awareness and sensitivity needed to build trusting relationships when working with children whose families, cultures, religions, and socioeconomic statuses differ from their own is a more complex process that teacher preparation and professional development programs often neglect to emphasize. Pia, who has been a preschool teacher for six years, works in a program serving diverse families, including immigrants from several countries. She spoke of how overwhelmed she feels during a discussion in her college class:

> I just want to teach and take care of children. But it's feeling really complicated and I'm not sure what to do anymore. I never expected to be dealing with parents battling over their children, families who don't speak English, children dealing with trauma, and coworkers who get angry every time I try to do something creative.

Pia feels that she understands what children need, but she sometimes finds that her perspectives are not shared by families and some of her colleagues. This is stressful for her because her background and training have not prepared her for the complicated issues she faces in her work. Understanding and relating to the ideas, expectations, and perspectives of strangers—including children, families, and colleagues—is a necessary skill. Teachers need practice cultivating skills and dispositions such as empathy, risk taking, and welcoming differences to provide high-quality care and education.

Can college classrooms become places where students such as Pia actively engage in learning the many skills required when caring for others? The shifting nature of today's college population may hold a key to this important new level of teacher preparation.

Who Goes to College?

Just as modern living has created circumstances that take families into a world of strangers, colleges are experiencing a similar diversification in their student population. Colleges now enroll many students who, by earlier standards, are considered nontraditional—students from a variety of socioeconomic backgrounds, students who speak English as a second language, working students, parents, immigrants, and older adults. These students make up about 74 percent of all US college and university undergraduates (NCES 2015).

Early childhood education is a popular field for many nontraditional students. Almost everyone can relate to facilitating children's learning and development on a personal level: through childhood experiences, parenthood, or having cared for the children of friends or family. This fits well with the supportive nature of the field. It also presents both challenges and opportunities for teacher educators.

Some teacher educators may find it challenging when the students they teach have different languages, cultures, lifestyles, and socioeconomic statuses from their own. An effective teacher educator views these diverse characteristics as strengths, crafts learning experiences that connect with students' lives, and creates a place where shared learning is valued. Fostering a nurturing environment enhances the level of education for all students, and it can be a model to encourage them to do the same for the children in their care.

Learning from Our Differences

We (Susan and Elizabeth) have spent many years exploring ways to create adult learning environments that support everyone, including nontraditional students (Bernheimer 2003, 2005; Exposito & Bernheimer 2012; Jones 1986, 2007). Our journey has brought us important insights into creating inclusive learning communities. We have discovered four critical factors needed to build communities for mutual learning:

> A nurturing environment

> Story sharing

> Reflective practice

> Open dialogue

A Nurturing Environment

The first college class I (Susan) taught was part of a program serving inner-city students who witnessed daily violence and lived with extreme economic hardships and unstable family lives. I realized that my standard teaching methods were not reaching the students. Almost everyone seemed anxious and uncomfortable being in the classroom. When I tried to give a lecture, the students seemed disconnected and withdrawn, or they talked loudly among themselves. My initial response was to blame the students—I had valuable information to give them, and they just didn't seem interested.

One day while lecturing on "healthy" families, I looked out at the class. Everybody appeared down and restless. Wanting the class to become more engaged, I asked them to share stories about healthy families they knew. Nobody raised a hand. Nobody would make eye contact with me. Looking around the room, I sensed the sadness and defeat they were feeling. Their lives and families did not fit the definition of *healthy* they heard me describe.

My usual way of teaching was alienating the students. Within the confines of standard definitions and theories, there was no place for them to see how both hardship and positive experiences can contribute to growth and learning. Taking a new approach, I asked, "How have you grown from a painful experience?" and "How have you grown from a positive experience?" These questions brought the class back to life. They could now share the truth of their lives as a valuable part of the learning process (Bernheimer 2003; Exposito & Bernheimer 2012; Palmer 2004).

Getting to Know the Students

Bringing the students' lives into classroom learning became a priority. I began by asking questions: "What are your concerns for your children? What challenges are you going through as primary caregivers?" Their responses were immediate. They became interested, paying close attention and expressing themselves. One morning, Jamie shared the following:

> My son is 8 years old. I watch over him all the time. I make sure he comes home every day right after school and does his homework. I'm scared all the time that he'll end up in a gang. And it's just too dangerous where I live to let him go out and play. I can't even take him to a safe park. But I'm worried that he isn't growing up right, just being inside all the time.

I acknowledged the importance of exploring the kind of issues Jamie shared from her life. Other students joined the conversation, telling their own stories and expressing empathy about her situation. Jamie's story had provided a way for them to connect personally with the educational process, validate their varied experiences, and be part of a supportive learning environment where all students could make a contribution (Belenky et al. 1986; Noddings 1991; Palmer 2004).

Responsiveness to Multiple Realities

By encouraging differing perspectives to become part of our learning experience, we all grew and learned from each other. The students' stories showed us that there is more than one right answer. The classroom was becoming a place where students could feel respected and understood. We were no longer strangers.

Just as children need a nurturing environment in which it is safe to learn and grow, so do adults. Maslow (1968) recognizes that new learning always requires taking the risk of letting go of the safety of previous conceptions. All human beings need acceptance and safety when faced with this risk. When students feel secure and comfortable expressing their experiences, we are preparing them to, in turn, understand others with differing perspectives, styles, ideas, and attitudes (Bernheimer 2005; Exposito & Bernheimer 2012).

Skills in Caring

A nurturing environment does more than provide the conditions for learning; it provides the basis for practicing the skills of caring. Noddings (2003) states that caring cannot be learned as theoretical information. It must be practiced in the classroom, using the communicative skills fundamental to caring relationships: listening, empathy, and being responsive to the needs of each person. Through empathetic listening and sharing of personal experiences in the class, we were all learning critical relational skills that early childhood educators need (Noddings 1991).

In our current educational climate, with increasing degree requirements and performance-based standards for teachers, it is tempting to eliminate time-consuming aspects of a curriculum such as sharing personal stories, reflecting, and carrying on a dialogue. Teacher preparation is based more on utilitarian calculations that create a mindset in which we do not consider the full humanity of others and the complexities of life. Students' personal stories include many hidden dimensions of experience, such as the memories, feelings, and circumstances of their lives.

I began selecting key topics from readings and designing the curriculum around students' stories. From our introductory exercise to specific course content, classroom activities, and homework assignments, sharing personal stories brought new levels of active participation and emotional connection (Bernheimer 2003; Noddings 1991).

Introductory Exercises

In a class focusing on children and diversity, I asked students to introduce themselves by sharing the story of their names. Their stories ranged from funny (being named after a cat his father had as a child) to complicated (hyphenated names mixing multiple cultures) to painful (named after her father who was killed in a war). An atmosphere of caring and respect among students and across cultures, races, and ethnicities began to emerge, and it grew with each story. For example, I watched a new awareness of cultural differences and of the often unseen struggles of immigrant children grow among the students as Lupita, an immigrant from Mexico, shared a story about her name. Her parents gave her a long and difficult-to-pronounce name. Typical of her culture, she was always called by a nickname. When she started kindergarten, the teacher called roll every day using her full name, but Lupita never recognized it and did not answer. Her parents and teacher got angry with her for not responding to her name. She remembered feeling invisible to everyone. By sharing these stories, we were taking our first steps in becoming a community.

Story Sharing

The early childhood education field offers many opportunities to include personal stories as a part of understanding the complexity of people's lives and development (Exposito & Bernheimer 2012). For this same course, I created a group activity in which students described their families while growing up, including positive and negative ways their families affected them and how their families were alike and different from one another's. I combined this with an outside assignment asking the students to do a case study of a family they considered very different from their own. Discussions from these assignments became very lively as they realized the vast differences in how children are reared and what is considered a family.

Allowing real-life issues to surface enabled students to look at patterns, contradictions, and inconsistencies in their lives and work (Wood 2000). For example, Mirabel shared her experience with Jorge, a 3-year-old child in the preschool program where she taught. Jorge refused to eat independently at mealtimes because his family always spoon-fed him. His teachers wanted him to work on feeding himself to help him develop self-care and fine motor skills. They kept trying to change this mealtime custom and became frustrated with his family. As a result of our class discussions, Mirabel had become more sensitive to cultural differences and decided to work with Jorge to bridge the cultural gap in this situation. She sat next to Jorge during meals, feeding him some and letting him slowly begin eating by himself. The students were learning to break through cultural differences and deepen their understanding of diverse histories and life choices.

Rosa, an immigrant from Guatemala who speaks English as a second language, describes her experience of sharing and listening to stories:

> It is a big difference of listening from everybody, from everybody's heart, from somebody's heart and tears, than reading it in a book—those learnings, you cannot

get them through the book. Because there is [only] so much you can picture in a book. You can read about your pain. But you will never see pain in those faces. And there was a time when somebody said, "Hey, you guys are doing great by trying hard." But the book will never tell you how hard you work. It won't ever say what is right in the book, because those people didn't write the book for people who speak some other language. (Bernheimer 2003, 72–73)

Reflective Practice

Early childhood educators respond to complicated and unexpected occurrences as part of their work, relying on their judgment rather than on prelearned answers. This skill requires much practice with multiple levels of learning, including self-awareness and understanding the often hidden reality of other people's lives. Reflections ranging from "the story of your name" to "how your family disciplined you" brought up surprising similarities and differences among the students. Most important, this process helped them learn that they can honor their own background while understanding and accepting those who are different.

For example, toddler teacher Ernesto knows the value of sand play for this age group, so the children he teaches spend a lot of time in the sandbox. One morning, he was approached by the mother of one of the children in his class, Sierra, who is 2 years old and African American. Sierra's mother was very upset and told Ernesto that she did not want her daughter to play in the sandbox anymore. He tried to explain the importance of sand play, but she said that if Sierra went in the sandbox again, she would withdraw her from the program. Shocked and confused, Ernesto didn't know what to do, but he wanted to understand the problem so that together, he and Sierra's mother might come up with a compromise or resolution. He asked if she could explain her concern, and Sierra's mother told him how difficult it is to get sand out of African American hair. Once Ernesto understood the problem, he suggested putting a shower cap over Sierra's hair when she played with sand. Her mother agreed.

When I realized that the textbooks and information from my lectures did not resonate with the real stories of the students' own journeys to this classroom, I created reflective assignments that invited them to examine and honor all of their experiences. Such reflections allowed them to make positive use of their life experiences (Bernheimer 2003).

I asked students to make observations in neighborhood parks, laundromats, schools, and their homes to give them practice in carefully observing the ways that many factors influence family–child interactions, including beliefs, culture, circumstances, and temperament. Within these familiar environments, they observed various aspects of children's and families' lives, such as temperament and discipline. They were learning to see both positive and negative interactions between families and children, and the effects of these interactions.

Open Dialogue

Early childhood educators engage in many dialogues every day with children, families, and colleagues. Open dialogue as part of a college curriculum provides an opportunity to develop this important skill. Class discussions focusing on topics that are relevant to students' lives promote their ability to accept ambiguity and see new possibilities in their perceptions of others.

In a group discussion about the challenges in communicating with families, students shared their frustrations with family members who do not come to family meetings and conferences. Listening to her peers, Marita added a different perspective by pointing out that her own mother never went to these meetings because she worked two jobs and could not speak English. Moments like these made the students pause and reflect on the biases and assumptions they were operating under and recognize circumstances they hadn't previously considered. Over time, the students moved away from the instinct to lay blame and learned to look more deeply at the needs of the person before them (Wood 2000).

Sharing their opinions also gave the students opportunities to take risks. This kind of risk taking is an essential trait for teachers of young children: "Teaching is a risky business. You never really know what will happen" (Jones 2007, 42). Teachers must be observant and reflective, and be able to work with ongoing assessment to determine whether their teaching practice is effective, and if so, how effective (Jones 2007).

During a literacy class for Head Start teachers, I observed the importance of dialogue among students. As we discussed setting up a lending library for families, Sonia said, "We have a large number of extra books to loan out, but none of the families will take them. They just don't seem interested in helping their children." Several class members added that they had had the same experience, so I asked the class, "Why do you think families aren't using the lending libraries?"

A lively discussion and varied opinions came forth, including "They don't want to sign their names on anything official with the school," "They're exhausted from working, commuting, and taking care of their children, and don't want anything else to deal with," and "They may not be able to read English and feel threatened." It was Irene who said, "Many don't want to sign their names because they cannot write. I started using stickers for them to place beside their names, and since then, I've had more families signing in to borrow books." This brought a wealth of ideas that teachers could use to make families feel comfortable using a lending library. It is through these kinds of mutual exchanges that students expand their perspectives and build skills for solving problems (West-Olatunji, Behar-Horenstein, & Rant 2008).

Conclusion

College classrooms can be ideal environments for early childhood educators to learn and practice the skills they need to recognize and appreciate people with backgrounds, ideas, and beliefs that are different from their own. In a supportive learning environment with active learning and reflective practices, being part of a diverse student population that has come together for a common purpose is a gift that adds to everyone's learning experiences.

Teacher educators can modify their teaching practices to be responsive to the backgrounds and life experiences of nontraditional students. When teachers ask students to share their stories, students teach us about the many important dimensions of learning and about their strengths, while validating them as capable learners (Bernheimer 2003; Exposito & Bernheimer 2012). Early childhood educators in Reggio Emilia, Italy, apply this same principle to children. By emphasizing the strengths found in any group of children, they have been powerful advocates for the rights of the child. Similarly, Paulo Freire (1998) became an advocate for oppressed adults in Brazil by teaching literacy using a pedagogy that acknowledges and builds on learners' diverse life experiences.

Adult learners, like young children, will be successful if they aren't expected to conform to a single set of teaching practices that might not be a good fit for who they are. The early childhood education field is built on the principle of inclusivity for all children. Incorporating the voices of student teachers as part of the learning process brings this inclusivity to nontraditional students. "Our role as college instructors isn't to screen people out of the early childhood profession. Our role is to invite them in, discovering and building on their strengths" (Jones 2007, 129).

Reflection Questions

1. This article identifies four factors that are needed to build communities of mutual learning: a nurturing environment, story sharing, reflective practice, and open dialogue. Which of these do you feel your program or classroom excel at? Which present a challenge?

2. What are some ways you currently (or plan to) help children learn from their differences? How have you (or can you) emphasize these differences as strengths?

3. Consider a time when you made a false assumption about someone else based on limited information (either in a personal or professional capacity). After reading this article, think about some steps you might have taken to help prevent this misunderstanding.

4. Think about a specific practice or routine in your classroom. How might you modify it to make it more engaging of and responsive to all children and families your program serves?

5. Have you ever had a situation where your beliefs about what would be developmentally appropriate for a specific child did not match his family's expectations? Knowing that developmentally appropriate practice requires attention to family and cultural expectations, how did you resolve the issue?

References

Belenky, M.F., B.M. Clinchy, N.R. Goldberger, & J.M. Tarule. 1986. *Women's Ways of Knowing: The Development of Self, Voice, and Mind*. New York: Basic Books.

Bernheimer, S. 2003. *New Possibilities for Early Childhood Education: Stories from Our Nontraditional Students*. New York: Peter Lang.

Bernheimer, S. 2005. "Telling Our Stories: A Key to Effective Teaching." *Exchange* 162 (March/April): 82–83.

BLS (US Department of Labor, Bureau of Labor Statistics). 2017. *Women in the Labor Force: A Databook*. Report 1071. Washington, DC: BLS. www.bls.gov/opub/reports/womens-databook/2017/pdf/home.pdf.

Child Care Aware of America. 2018. *What Does Child Care Look Like in Your State?—2018 State Fact Sheets*. Report. Arlington, VA: Child Care Aware of America. www.usa.childcareaware.org/wp-content/uploads /2018/08/2018-state-fact-sheets.pdf.

Exposito, S., & S. Bernheimer. 2012. "Nontraditional Students and Institutions of Higher Education: A Conceptual Framework." *Journal of Early Childhood Teacher Education* 33 (2): 178–89.

Freire, P. 1998. "Pedagogy of the Oppressed: The Fear of Freedom." In *The Paulo Freire Reader*, eds. A.M.A. Freire & D.P. Macedo, 45–66. New York: Continuum.

Jones, E. 1986. *Teaching Adults: An Active Learning Approach*. Washington, DC: NAEYC.

Jones, E. 2007. *Teaching Adults Revisited: Active Learning for Early Childhood Educators*. Washington, DC: NAEYC.

Laughlin, L. 2013. "Who's Minding the Kids? Child Care Arrangements: Spring 2011." *Household Economic Studies*. Washington, DC: US Census Bureau. www.census.gov/prod/2013pubs/p70-135.pdf.

Maslow, A. 1968. *Toward a Psychology of Being*. New York: Van Nostrand Reinhold.

NCES (US Department of Education, National Center for Education Statistics). 2015. *Demographic and Enrollment Characteristics of Nontraditional Undergraduates: 2011–12*. Report NCES 2015-025. Washington, DC: NCES. www.nces.ed.gov/pubs2015/2015025.pdf.

Noddings, N. 1991. "Stories in Dialogue: Caring and Interpersonal Reasoning." In *Stories Lives Tell: Narrative and Dialogue in Education*, eds. C. Witherell & N. Noddings, 157–70. New York: Teachers College Press.

Noddings, N. 2003. *Caring: A Feminine Approach to Ethics and Moral Education*. 2nd ed. Berkeley: University of California Press.

Palmer, P.J. 2004. *A Hidden Wholeness: The Journey Toward an Undivided Life*. San Francisco: Jossey-Bass.

West-Olatunji, C., L. Behar-Horenstein, & J. Rant. 2008. "Mediated Lesson Study, Collaborative Learning, and Cultural Competence Among Early Childhood Educators." *Journal of Research in Childhood Education* 23 (1): 96–108.

Wood, D.R. 2000. "Narrating Professional Development: Teachers' Stories as Texts for Improving Practice." *Anthropology and Education Quarterly* 31 (4): 426–48.

About the Authors

Susan Bernheimer, PhD, is an educator and consultant on modern issues facing early childhood education. She was a faculty member in human development at Pacific Oaks College in Pasadena, California. Susan was also an instructor for college programs serving students in poverty for 10 years.

Elizabeth Jones, PhD, is faculty emerita in human development at Pacific Oaks College. She is the author of *Teaching Adults Revisited: Active Learning for Early Childhood Educators* (NAEYC, 2007) and other books on play and emergent curriculum.

Photographs: pp. 5, 6, 7, 8, 9, 11, 12, 13, 14, © Getty Images

Moving Beyond Anti-Bias Activities
Supporting the Development of Anti-Bias Practices

Lisa P. Kuh, Debbie LeeKeenan, Heidi Given, and Margaret R. Beneke

"My dad is thiiiiiis black!"

"Why does she wear that scarf on her head?"

"My mom makes me give toys I don't like to poor kids who don't have any."

"Only girls can be nurses."

These comments, while typical of young children, can stop a teacher in her tracks. How should teachers respond? Children's comments can sometimes fluster both new and experienced teachers—even those who support equity and diversity in schools. While teaching at the Eliot-Pearson Children's School at Tufts University, we authors explored what it means to embrace an anti-bias stance every day. We found that adopting an anti-bias perspective requires more than implementing a few well-meaning activities. Instead, doing so asks educators to think differently about their work, take personal and professional risks, and put new ideas and beliefs into practice. The teachers at Eliot-Pearson developed a framework to guide their anti-bias work and support their anti-bias planning and practice as they moved forward.

What Is Anti-Bias Education?

Anti-bias education is a way of teaching that supports children and their families as they develop a sense of identity and fairness in a highly diverse and still inequitable society. It helps children learn to be proud of themselves and their families, respect a range of human differences, recognize unfairness and bias, and speak up for the rights of others (Derman-Sparks & Edwards 2010).

Children tell us every day through their comments, play, and peer interactions that they notice social issues, are curious about differences, and want more information. So what do schools and teachers need to do? In many ways, anti-bias education may not be so different from the kind of teaching that educators already do. For example, when children notice butterflies in the garden, teachers might notice and respond to children's curiosity as an

A Closer Look at Anti-Bias Education

Early childhood educators believe in the principle that all people deserve the opportunities and resources to fulfill their complete humanity. Educators have a unique role in making this principle real by promoting all children's chances to thrive in school, in work, and in life. Anti-bias education is a catalyst for empowerment of children, authentic engagement of families, and hope for staff that they can truly make a meaningful difference in early childhood programs.

Why Is Anti-Bias Work Important?

We live in a world that is not yet a place where all children have equal opportunities to become all they are and can be. We do anti-bias work because we see what happens when children receive messages about themselves that do not support their personal and social identities, or their intelligence and competency. We do it because we see the injury to children when adults become silent in the face of children teasing or rejecting others because of who they are. We do it because we want a world in which all children are able to blossom, and each child's particular abilities and gifts are able to flourish. To thrive in a diverse and inequitable world, all children need

> **A positive sense of self.** How does the world think of me and my family? How do I think and feel about myself and my family?

> **Connection to others.** Who are you? How are we alike? How are we different?

> **Fairness.** What is fair or unfair? What hurts me? What hurts other people?

> **Empowerment.** How can I stand up for myself? How can I stand up for others? How can we change unfair to fair?

The Four Core Goals of Anti-Bias Education

The core goals and educational principles of anti-bias education foster all children's abilities to thrive. All four are essential to an effective anti-bias education program.

Goal 1: Identity

Each child will demonstrate self-awareness, confidence, family pride, and positive personal and social identities. Children's personal identities are shaped by their multiple social group identities. Positive self-concept is foundational to children's development in all aspects of school and life.

Guidelines for Teaching this Goal

> Make visible and support each child's specific social identities in the classroom environment, in the curriculum, and in all social interactions.

> Nurture children's sense of self, which is centered in the social identities of their families, by treating each family with respect and care.

Goal 2: Diversity

Each child will express comfort and joy with human diversity; accurate language for human differences; and deep, caring human connections. Understanding that we are all different and the same is central. Children learn prejudice from prejudice—not from learning about human diversity. It is how people respond to differences that teaches bias and fear.

opportunity for extending curriculum, and then provide books and other materials about life cycles. But when it comes to talking about race, class, gender, family structure, or ability, teachers might consciously, or even unconsciously, avoid elaborating on these topics.

Anti-bias curriculum topics often come from the children, families, and teachers, as well as from historical or current events. Anti-bias education happens in both planned curriculum and natural teachable moments based on children's conversations and play. Teachers have to balance planned anti-bias teaching experiences, such as exploring the way girls and boys can be both physically strong and kind, with seizing emergent opportunities to engage children by responding to their questions and observations. Anti-bias education calls on teachers to examine their own experiences, beliefs, and assumptions in order to push past the misinformation and biases that keep us from

Guidelines for Teaching this Goal

> Explore the ideas that we share similar attributes and needs (e.g., the need for food, shelter, and love; the commonalities of language, families, and feelings) and we live these in many different ways. Support children's cognitive and emotional growth with rich vocabulary about human differences and sameness.

> Talk about the many kinds of diversity present among the children in the group, even when they come from similar racial, cultural, economic class, and family backgrounds.

> Acquaint children with groups of people who live and work in their neighborhood and city. Preschoolers learn best about people as individuals.

Goal 3: Justice

Each child will increasingly recognize unfairness, have language to describe unfairness, and understand that unfairness hurts. For children to construct a strong self-concept or develop respect for others, they also must know how to identify and resist hurtful, stereotypical, and inaccurate messages or actions directed toward them or others.

Guidelines for Teaching this Goal

> Pay attention to the stereotypes and biases in the larger world and observe children's play behavior and comments to see where they are confused or fearful or misinformed. Engage in clarifying conversations and set limits on hurtful behaviors.

> Help children learn how to contrast inaccurate, untrue images or ideas with accurate ones.

> Help children expand their understanding of how people are hurt by stereotyping and unfair treatment.

Goal 4. Empowerment

Each child will demonstrate empowerment and the skills to act, with others or alone, against prejudice and/or discriminatory actions. If a child or a child's peer is not treated fairly, no child can feel safe. Even very young children can learn and practice ways to act when others are behaving in a biased manner or an unfair situation arises.

Guidelines for Teaching this Goal

> Engage children in dialogue about their feelings and ideas regarding unfair situations. Provide accurate information about the situation.

> With the children, plan and carry out actions to change unfair to fair.

Stop and Think: Imagine

Because of societal inequities, too many children still do not have access to the basic human rights due to them. Imagine a world of justice and equal opportunity for *all*.

> How would the world look different for each of the children you work with?

> How would the world look different for the program you work in?

(Adapted from Derman-Sparks & Edwards 2010, forthcoming)

noticing how an early childhood program may be undermining some children's identities and reinforcing hurtful stereotypes. As stated in NAEYC's Code of Ethics, accreditation materials, and position statements, supporting children's family identities and sense of safety and belonging is fundamental in our work.

Creating a Framework for Anti-Bias Teaching

The Eliot-Pearson Children's School's long-standing commitment to anti-bias education is part of its core values and mission. However, being intentional about anti-bias education across classrooms wasn't always easy. One year, as a curriculum strategy, each classroom focused on a particular issue related to its group of children. The teachers shared documentation and questions about this focus at monthly professional development meetings, receiving and giving feedback on curriculum and teaching practices. Topics included same-sex parents, skin color and racial identity, class and power, abilities and challenges, and cultural backgrounds.

To hold themselves accountable for anti-bias work, the program's teachers developed a tool for keeping anti-bias issues alive in the curriculum (see "Framework for Anti-Bias Teaching" on page 21). The work of three of this article's coauthors—Lisa (pre-K), Heidi (kindergarten), and Margaret (mixed-age first and second grade)—illustrates curriculum development prompted by the framework and support for anti-bias work for individual teachers and for the school as a whole. The framework has been modified further and discussed in more detail in *Leading Anti-Bias Early Childhood Programs: A Guide for Change* (Derman-Sparks, LeeKeenan, & Nimmo 2015).

Entry Points

Entry points include identifying, provoking, or uncovering themes that children are thinking about or demonstrating in their play. An entry point may be something a family brings to a teacher's attention or something a teacher knows about a family that a child brings to the setting. It may be a topic in the media—such as an election, a demonstration, or a film—that draws attention to a particular issue. In addition to recognizing entry points, educators

Framework for Anti-Bias Teaching	
Entry points What are children, teachers, and families thinking about?	Consider what you ❯ See in children's play ❯ See in the news ❯ Hear families talking about ❯ Think about yourself ❯ Need to do to listen carefully to children and families ❯ Might document to determine possible entry points
Feeling What feelings come up for you?	Consider how you ❯ Feel initially ❯ React initially ❯ Respond based on your personal experiences ❯ Feel about discussing a topic with children or families
Thinking What might be meaningful to explore with the children?	Consider planning ❯ Individually ❯ With your team ❯ With colleagues ❯ By doing more research about a topic ❯ By analyzing and reviewing documentation ❯ Whether an issue feels appropriate to discuss with the program's children and families
Responding How do you implement a curriculum that supports learning?	Consider how you could ❯ Respond in the moment ❯ Respond long-term ❯ Revisit or expand on the issue with children ❯ Make topics accessible to children
Sharing How do you share anti-bias learning by communicating process and outcomes?	Consider the ways you can share with ❯ Children ❯ Teachers (each other) ❯ Families ❯ Colleagues ❯ The early childhood education field

should understand that their responses to children's queries don't have to be instantaneous. They may not know right away how to respond—or whether they even want to explore a particular issue with a group—but the awareness of the topic is an important first step. Identification of entry points is at the beginning of the road map for curriculum planning. It takes place with the understanding that anti-bias issues raised are not problems to be eliminated but rather opportunities for teaching and learning.

Margaret's First- and Second-Grade Class

In this mixed-age inclusive class, teachers hear children saying things like "That's not fair! She gets an easier sheet than me!," "Why does he get to use a rocking chair at meetings? Can I?," and "I am bad at reading." Margaret knows that children's notions of fairness and their perceptions of themselves and others as learners provide entry points to rich conversations. Differences and similarities in ability are part of a conversation that starts on the very first day of school.

Heidi's Kindergarten Class

When Heidi hears kindergartners say, "This is my ramp. This is a private ramp," and "You can go up any ramp, if you have a lot of money. People with a lot of money can go in anywhere they want," she realizes that children are thinking about issues of ownership, resources, and power. This "a-ha!" moment inspires her to pay close attention to the language and understandings children have about social class, wealth, and privilege. As the kindergartners play, she notes that the children's attempts to assert themselves often reference possession ("I got it first"), ownership ("That's mine"), status ("I am the boss"), and cultural capital ("If you don't know this movie, then you don't know how to play").

Lisa's Pre-K Class

For sharing time, 4-year-old Julian, who is biracial, shows photographs of an experiment he did at home in which he added cream to his mother's coffee to try to match the color of his own skin. Later, 4-year-old Tywanna tells her lunch tablemates, "I'm lucky because my mom is light and my dad is dark and I am in the middle—a mix!" Hearing this, Lisa and her teaching team realize that the children are grappling with racial identity. The teachers decide to work with the class to help children learn language to talk about race together.

Feeling

For each potential entry point, it is important for educators to identify their feelings related to the anti-bias issue. Teachers may not necessarily know who to talk to about their feelings, and often this is where they get stuck. Their personal experiences may drive their responses, or they may experience discomfort and ignore the topic altogether. For example, Heidi felt overwhelmed and dismayed at the play she observed, based on her own class background. Teachers often change the subject when anti-bias topics come up or redirect children to distract them from the topic at hand. At Eliot-Pearson, this framework helps teachers address ambivalent feelings they have about a topic. Discussing their feelings about a topic with colleagues can help educators gain clarity about how to manage the curriculum.

Margaret's First- and Second-Grade Class

Margaret is upset that the children in her classroom are using ability to gain social power. It bothers her that differentiating curriculum based on children's skill levels seems to be provoking competition among them, sometimes hindering their self-confidence and willingness to take academic risks. Margaret worries that by exploring and discussing abilities, some of the children will feel singled out by their differences. Would asking the children to admit that they are challenged by some assignments be comfortable or productive? Would a particular child with obvious physical differences be able to participate in the conversation, or would classmates see him as a mascot for inclusion rather than an equal member of the class?

Heidi's Kindergarten Class

Heidi struggles with the connections she sees between kindergartners' play and issues of access, possession, and power present in our society. While she feels excited and nervous as the children explore social class concepts, she also worries about approaching a subject that seems taboo even in adult conversation. As she explores her own feelings, she wonders, "What role do teachers play that might be supporting and reinforcing ideas of ownership as power? How do our own class backgrounds affect perceptions of children, and how might our backgrounds equip us, or not, to support the children as they expand their understanding of these ideas?"

Thinking

Once the teachers at Eliot-Pearson considered entry points that identified areas of interest to the children and acknowledged their own feelings, they got down to the business of thinking about potential next steps. Documentation is crucial in inspiring teachers' thinking. The documentation process involves raising questions and closely observing, collecting, and recording information on children's experiences. Teachers can take photographs, listen to and record audio of children's conversations, and observe and record videos of children's play. They can continue to bring questions to colleagues, using the documentation to ask questions such as "What are these children working on and why?" and "What can I do in my classroom to support children's exploration and understanding of this topic?"

Initially, the kindergarten teaching team was stuck—unsure about how to explore ideas of possession and power with children this young. Teachers shared their thinking with families and colleagues, learning about the values they thought were important. Teachers began to look at power as a way to consider acts of sharing and giving (rather than having and holding)—encouraging the children to "use their powers for good." They developed activities that asked children to think about times when they had used possession or ownership to assert power, and to generate possible solutions to fairly distributing and sharing classroom resources and materials.

Lisa's Pre-K Class

Lisa and the pre-K teaching team review Julian's coffee photographs and, with his parents' knowledge and permission, talk with him further to explore the motivation behind his experiment. He uses a term—mulatto—to describe himself as someone who is mixed race. The teachers know that this term is widely considered to be an offensive racial slur in the United States. They feel uncomfortable hearing and using the term, and they recognize this as an opportunity to apply the goals of anti-bias education. This includes engaging Julian's family in a respectful conversation in order to understand Julian's use of this term as well as talking with all the children about using unbiased words to describe themselves and others.

Teachers begin keeping track of children's conversations about race and skin color at play, lunch, and group meetings. Children's comments reveal confusion about what the terms *White* and *Black* really mean in relation to skin color. They point to each other's clothing, noting that someone has white pants or a black shirt. As a result, the teachers think about ways to broaden and clarify skin color vocabulary.

Responding

Much of the work up until this phase involved observing, reflecting, documenting, and questioning. In the responding phase, teachers plan and implement intentional, specific experiences. Teachers choose curriculum changes to implement in the moment and through long-term planning. Again, documentation plays a part, as analysis of children's conversations can help teachers choose what to respond to and how to respond. Teachers also offer children the skills and tools they need for specific learning experiences. Consider the butterfly example mentioned earlier; teachers might give children opportunities to explore with magnifying glasses and clipboards before heading out into the garden. Providing children with initial materials and experiences can support their later engagement with deeper content. With anti-bias curriculum, these guided experiences might occur by simply mixing various colors of paint before beginning to explore skin colors.

Margaret's First- and Second-Grade Class

Over the course of two months, Margaret invites visitors into her classroom to teach and share information about many kinds of differences in ability, including physical, sensory, social, emotional, communication, and cognitive. An assistive technology teacher shows the children how some people who are developing expressive language skills use computers to help them communicate their ideas. A local university student tells the children about her own reading challenges and shares a strategy she uses for tracking words on a page. A former student with vision impairment engages the children by using humor and animating his voice as he tells a story. Margaret and the children create a classroom book documenting these conversations with visitors. As they revisit the book, they reflect on the idea that everyone has things they are great at and things they are working on. The children ultimately include pages about their own abilities and challenges. One child writes, "I am great at math problems. One thing that is challenging is waiting and raising my hand."

Heidi's Kindergarten Class

During a planning session, the kindergarten teachers identify three phrases that are commonly used during the children's negotiation of play: "But I got that first. It's mine," "I have the [toy], so I have to be the boss," and "We should have a rule that the person who has a thing decides the rules for the thing." Heidi talks to the children about these phrases. Children and teachers spend two meetings telling stories about times when these phrases were used to assert power over others. Heidi then presents a provocation: "Should we use the words we talked about at our meeting when we use the bikes?" The children immediately chorus, "No, no. Those rules are no good. They're not fair." Over the next three weeks, the kindergartners debate and develop a plan for sharing the bikes and wagons, which includes having a sign-up sheet for taking turns and considering the needs of preschoolers, who are often passengers.

Lisa's Pre-K Class

Lisa and the preschool team (two White teachers and one Black teacher) spend weeks engaging with the children in sensory- and art-inspired paint-mixing activities. In doing so, the children move beyond the novelty of color mixing to focus on systematically producing a color close to their own skin. Children name their various skin color shades—*bologna* being the most notable! Children also dramatize the Rosa Parks story to talk about *White* and *Black* as terms attributed to whole groups of people who really aren't that exact color, and they discuss the exclusionary practices associated with those terms.

Sharing: Process and Outcomes

Teachers at the Eliot-Pearson Children's School regularly use documentation to make learning visible to children, families, and school visitors (Krechevsky et al. 2013). The teachers in these scenarios also wanted to share what was happening with the anti-bias work, and they created documentation to show the scope and depth of the children's learning. The school year culminated in an anti-bias exhibition and gallery walk that was open to the public. Each classroom team made a documentation board that illustrated the different sections of the framework and shared key outcomes of the children's experiences. Visitors could share questions and comments and add their own ideas by responding to several interactive bulletin boards through writing messages on sticky notes.

Margaret's First- and Second-Grade Class

Having documented classroom learning and shared the anti-bias work with families and school visitors, Margaret and her team now feel more comfortable discussing abilities and addressing unfair language in the classroom. Margaret notes the increase in children's use of the phrases "what he's [or she's] working on" and "just right" work to explain why different children have different assignments. Children share their diverse abilities with each other by writing comments on sticky notes in response to each other's pages in the classroom book. Margaret notes how children are able to take more academic risks and how she differentiates tasks in heterogeneous skill groups more flexibly, often referencing the classroom book when differences arise.

Heidi's Kindergarten Class

The long-term planning time and subsequent use of the sign-up sheet enable kindergartners to plan for using classroom and school resources and to express and negotiate roles, story lines, and connections rather than arguing over who gets a turn and who gets to control the play. Teachers experiment with different ways to dismiss children at choice times, so that no one "got there first." Teachers' efforts to change some classroom structures, in tandem with the plans made for sharing bikes, support teamwork and problem solving in play.

Lisa's Pre-K Class

The preschoolers share their learning by inviting families and friends to visit the classroom and participate in mixing paint to match their own skin colors. With the children as expert color mixers, the classroom visitors create their skin color, experiencing the expanded vocabulary about race that the children developed. On their gallery walk panel, Lisa presents information from research about race so families can see how it connects to the work in the classroom.

Conclusion

It is important to note that throughout this exploration of anti-bias topics, the teachers at the Eliot-Pearson Children's School had some key structures in place that were vital to their ability to sustain the hard work of reflective teaching, especially as related to potentially controversial topics. The following structures were included:

> **Make a commitment to anti-bias work.** The school made anti-bias education a primary focus and was dedicated to trying out new ideas; integrating theory, research, and practice; and building a culture that allowed risk taking and making mistakes—essential components of anti-bias education. For some teachers—even those familiar with anti-bias work—their understandings of this approach broadened. One teacher reflected, "I initially thought anti-bias was about race, but I see that it can incorporate many different types of bias." Another teacher said, "I realized how frequently spontaneous teaching moments occur in the classroom. I became a better listener and was able to use everyday situations as prompts for future whole group discussions."

> **Use tools for staying on track.** Having a tool such as the framework for anti-bias teaching supported educators as they learned to consider anti-bias issues in deeper, more holistic, and intentional ways. It also held teachers accountable for keeping anti-bias education in the forefront of their teaching repertoire—implementing purposeful curriculum to move the work in the classroom forward. The framework became a filter

through which teachers could discuss, plan, and gauge their work. A second teacher noted, "I feel it is important to be intentional about discussions of difference—that way children are given language and support and teachers are not caught unprepared." Additionally, the framework gave voice to new ways of thinking for teachers and children. One teacher reflected, "Children need language and experiences to broaden their understanding of diversity. The more experiences they have, the more easily they can take an anti-bias approach themselves."

> **Gain administrative support and dedicated meeting time for anti-bias education work.** Making anti-bias education a priority for curriculum development and professional development means providing time, funds, and resources to this effort. Debbie LeeKeenan, the director of the school, made a conscious decision to dedicate staff meeting time to anti-bias work and, as a result, teachers were engaged in monthly professional development sharing and received regular feedback on anti-bias dilemmas. Teachers used a model of collaboration and specific protocols to guide their conversations and review dilemmas and the children's work. As a result, teachers saw staff meetings as a place to "take our data and elicit feedback and reflection from colleagues, which influences our continued implementation of the curriculum." This kind of embedded professional development created trust among teachers and was an important venue for sharing entry points, feelings, thinking, and planning.

Working through the movements of the framework can bring up feelings of discomfort and move teachers to question which topics are introduced and how they are covered in their teaching practices. One teacher admitted, "It is still so hard to set priorities and decide what aspects of all the potential discussions get my attention, air time, group time, and curricular development." But teachers were also adamant that the work was worth the effort. Another teacher expressed it this way: "I am a learner too. Curriculum should be about actively exploring a topic with each other. I learned that part of our job as teachers is to aid children and families in areas they may be struggling with. Though our ideas and beliefs may differ, it is still our job to negotiate through these."

Doing this work was not always easy, but it was rich, it shifted practice, and ultimately it was satisfying. Observing children as they have their own "a-ha!" moments—noticing an injustice, developing a new connection to a peer, or building an understanding of the world around them and their own role in making the world a more just place—is inspiring. It is equally satisfying to teachers to have taken a risk and stretched our own learning as a means to provide a deeper and more inclusive education for all.

Reflection Questions

1. How do you feel when you hear a child make a comment that could be construed as racially charged or that you are not sure how to handle? What do you do?

2. Examine the headings in the "Framework for Anti-Bias Teaching" figure on page 21. Which step do you think best matches your development as an educator? At which step might you encounter the most challenges?

3. What anti-bias issues are currently being discussed in your center, school, or community? How might these issues impact your work with children?

4. How might your identity and personal history impact your perception of children, including who they are and what they can and should do as part of their learning experiences, especially as related to anti-bias topics?

5. Because of societal inequities, too many children still do not have access to the basic human rights due them. Imagine a world of justice and equal opportunity for all. How would the world look different for each of the children you work with? How would the world look different for the program you work in?

References

Derman-Sparks, L., & J.O. Edwards. 2010. *Anti-Bias Education for Young Children and Ourselves.* Washington, DC: NAEYC.

Derman-Sparks, L., & J.O. Edwards. Forthcoming. *Anti-Bias Education for Young Children and Ourselves.* 2nd ed. Washington, DC: NAEYC.

Derman-Sparks, L., D. LeeKeenan, & J. Nimmo. 2015. *Leading Anti-Bias Early Childhood Programs: A Guide for Change.* New York: Teachers College Press; Washington, DC: NAEYC.

Krechevsky, M., B. Mardell, M. Rivard, & D. Wilson. 2013. *Visible Learners: Promoting Reggio-Inspired Approaches in All Schools.* San Francisco: Jossey Bass.

Resources

Husband, T. 2012. "'I Don't See Color': Challenging Assumptions About Discussing Race with Young Children." *Early Childhood Education Journal* 39 (6): 365–71.

Segura-Mora, A. 2008. "What Color Is Beautiful?" In *Rethinking Early Childhood Education,* ed. A. Pelo, 3–6. Milwaukee, WI: Rethinking Schools.

About the Authors

Lisa P. Kuh, PhD, is director of early education for Somerville Public Schools, in Somerville, Massachusetts, and an adjunct professor at Lesley University. She was previously an assistant professor at the University of New Hampshire, as well as a teacher, lecturer, and researcher at the Eliot-Pearson Children's School and Department of Child Development at Tufts University.

Debbie LeeKeenan, MA, is an early childhood consultant and lecturer. From 1996 to 2013, she was director of the Eliot-Pearson Children's School. Debbie is coauthor of From Survive to Thrive: A Director's Guide for Leading an Early Childhood Program (NAEYC, 2018) and *Leading Anti-Bias Early Childhood Programs: A Guide for Change* (Teachers College Press; NAEYC 2015).

Heidi Given, MA, is an early childhood instructional coach based in Somerville, Massachusetts. She has worked as a mentor teacher in a variety of school settings, including public and charter schools, Head Start programs, center-based programs, and university lab schools. Heidi is an adjunct lecturer at Lesley University as well as a founder and facilitator of the Early Childhood Professional Development Consortium.

Margaret R. Beneke, PhD, is assistant professor at the University of Washington's College of Education. Her research focuses on increasing access to inclusive, equitable education for children and families from historically marginalized backgrounds. Margaret's work has been published in a number of journals, including *Journal of Early Childhood Literacy, Topics in Early Childhood Special Education,* and *Early Childhood Education Journal.*

Capitalizing on Culture

Engaging Young Learners in Diverse Classrooms

Tyrone C. Howard

Diversity remains a heartbeat of the US way of life. Perhaps no place reflects the manner in which racial, ethnic, linguistic, and cultural diversity are manifested better than the nation's public schools (Banks 2015). To grasp the unprecedented demographic transformation that the nation is currently experiencing, consider that as of the fall of 2014, for the first time in the nation's history, there was a higher number of non-White children enrolling in US schools than White children (NCES 2017). This important shift had been predicted by demographers for some time; still, it represented a milestone in racial and cultural dynamics in the country's schools and was a watershed moment in the changing makeup of the nation that will continue over time. The demographic transformation comes as the nation's public schools have enrolled surging numbers of Latino/a and Asian American children in recent years. According to the National Center for Education Statistics (NCES 2017), Latino/a children accounted for 25 percent of US public elementary and secondary students in the fall of 2014 and are projected to make up close to 30 percent of students by the fall of 2026. Hence, ethnic, racial, and cultural diversity is a staple of our nation's schools—and it is a strength as we try to live up to our core democratic ideals.

As diversity increases in the nation's schools, the prevalence of student punishment and discipline is an area that concerns many. What has become increasingly apparent is that the greater the ethnic and racial diversity in schools, the higher the rates of disciplinary action (Skiba et al. 2015). Disproportionate expulsions and suspensions of African American and Latino/a children in particular, along with their placement in special education classes, remain normative practices in many school districts, even among the youngest of learners (Artiles et al. 2010; Gilliam et al. 2016; Harry & Klingner 2014). A number of scholars have raised the possibility that cultural misunderstandings, racial discrimination, and implicit bias may all contribute to this problem, all of which seem to have gotten worse since the beginning of the 21st century (Howard 2010).

A report released by the Office for Civil Rights (OCR) in 2014 revealed distinct differences in school discipline for children across racial and cultural lines. The OCR data indicate that the discipline disparities start early and continue throughout the school experiences of racially diverse students. African Americans make up 18 percent of all preschool age children, yet they comprised almost 50 percent of all preschoolers who received out-of-school suspensions in 2012 (OCR 2014). One can only question what offenses could lead to the suspension of 4- and 5-year-old children, but for Black children, it's happening frequently across the nation.

To underscore disproportionality in discipline measures among young learners, recent research examining suspension of preschoolers discovered that many preschool teachers and staff administer discipline in ways that often disadvantage Black students (Gilliam et al. 2016). The teachers' races play a big role in disciplinary actions, with White teachers disciplining Black children with greater frequency than Black teachers. This research also suggests that White educators may be acting on stereotypes, such as that Black preschoolers are more likely to misbehave, effectively judging Black and White children against different standards. While more research is needed, it appears that many early childhood educators expect worse behavior from, and have lower learning expectations for, Black children than for other children.

Given the increasing racial and cultural diversity in the nation's schools, and in early childhood programs in particular, what role should cultural relevance have in teaching practices and policy? What are the essential knowledge and skills that early childhood educators need for teaching today's diverse learners? And how are learning prospects compromised for diverse learners when educators do not understand them culturally? It is vital for early childhood educators to develop cultural awareness and essential proficiencies to effectively teach across racial and cultural differences. Understanding the cultural capital of young learners moves practitioners away from believing there are deficits and pathologies among communities, children, and families of color (Bloom, Davis, & Hess 1965; Moynihan 1965) and toward seeing children's behaviors through a cultural asset lens (Gay 2010). Hence, a fundamental approach to understanding the cultural capital of young learners is to recognize that *different* ways of doing, knowing, communicating, learning, and living do not mean *deficient.*

Cultural Capital and Young Learners

To fully comprehend cultural capital, it is essential to grasp the concept of culture. As researcher Fred Erickson notes, "The term *culture* is slippery in meaning" (2012, 4). He states that "everybody is multicultural" (16) and that

> although important cultural learning occurs in early childhood, such learning continues across the life span; . . . individuals within named social groups differ culturally . . . [as] the result of their participation in differing local communities of cultural practice . . . in which they live their daily lives. (16)

Erickson's notion of "local communities of cultural practice" is a helpful reminder of the personal yet social nature of culture; it encompasses the norms, practices, beliefs, systems, and structures that guide daily living for individuals. This is vital for early childhood educators to understand when working with diverse learners. In short, culture matters.

The importance of culture in the learning process cannot be overstated. For example, much of the curriculum, instructional approaches, and assessment mechanisms in US schools are steeped in mainstream (i.e., Eurocentric) ideology, language, norms, and examples, while non-White ways of knowing and being are often excluded (Gay 2010; Howard 2010). For example, among many Black students, participation can be very spontaneous and demonstrative, kinship bonds are highly valued, and connecting academic content to prior cultural knowledge is essential (Boykin 1986; Milner 2010; Nasir 2011). This is not to suggest that these factors are not also critical for White students. Yet in many preschool learning settings, the expectations for how to perform or behave in school lack cultural nuances that many non-White students depend on for participation and engagement in learning. Eurocentric approaches in schools, even for young learners, prioritize certain ways of talking, learning, sharing, and participating that may be foreign to many children of color. Moreover, books and activities that rarely reflect the experiences, stories, sayings,

parables, backgrounds, and histories of children of color can also lead to disengagement and refusal to participate in learning (Bishop 2007).

It is vital for early childhood educators to develop a firm grasp of how students' cultural capital influences the ways students think, speak, process, and make meaning of school situations and circumstances. Education scholar Gloria Ladson-Billings stated over two decades ago that culture matters in teaching and learning because culturally relevant approaches are "a pedagogy that empowers students intellectually, socially, emotionally, and politically by using cultural referents to impart knowledge, skills, and attitudes" (1995, 382). Teaching approaches should not denigrate the use of nonstandard English;

instead, they should pay attention to children's social and emotional realities outside of school and affirm students' unique ways of contributing to learning. Being intellectually empowering means recognizing, and even encouraging and praising, children's creativity in expressing what they know; it also means recognizing their prior knowledge as important and necessary to learning new information. Moreover, instructional approaches that are politically meaningful are based on teachers' recognition that even for preschoolers and other young learners, making age-appropriate references to relevant issues in communities where children live and learn can be critical as well. Asking children to talk about what they see in their neighborhoods—people, colors, places, buildings, stores, and the overall environment— can stimulate them to make connections between new learning and familiar knowledge. Incorporating age-appropriate multicultural literature can also be valuable for teachers who are not familiar with the backgrounds of some diverse learners.

Wanting to increase recognition of all students' cultural capital, education scholar Tara Yosso (2005) developed a conceptual framework that she terms the Community Cultural Wealth model, which recognizes the skills, strengths, and experiences that children of color bring with them to the classroom environment. Yosso's model is intended to help teachers use a strengths-based perspective to understand how students of color access information and learn. She breaks down the broad concept of cultural capital into six types of capital: (1) aspirational, (2) linguistic, (3) familial, (4) social, (5) navigational, and (6) resistant. The brief explanations that follow include prompts for thinking about ways to incorporate children's knowledge and strengths into the curriculum.

1. **Aspirational capital** consists of the ambitions, dreams, and hopes that children and families of color possess—and their abilities to foster those desires even in the midst of adversity and hopelessness. Many non-White children, like their White peers, and their families have high educational aspirations despite encountering persistent inequities (especially long-term economic and educational barriers) while pursuing these goals and personal, educational, and professional accomplishments.

   Questions to consider:

   > How do teachers create space, time, and opportunities in their classrooms to encourage and develop children to share, explore, and discuss their aspirations?

   > What learning arrangements do teachers offer children to share and nurture their aspirations as they develop literacy, numeracy, and social-emotional skills?

2. **Linguistic capital** is the comprehensive set of language and interaction skills that children possess as a result of their communication experiences. For many children of color, the role of oral and written storytelling, *pláticas*, fables, sayings, and age-old phrases in their homes and communities is an essential component of linguistic capital.

   Questions to consider:

   > How are teachers identifying, scaffolding, and supporting the development of all children's diverse language and communication variations, uniqueness, and strengths?

   > How are teachers creating classroom spaces and pedagogical approaches that recognize, embrace, and build on the diverse linguistic orientations that all students bring to the classroom?

3. **Familial capital** refers to the cultural and communal knowledge and ways of knowing and being that are nurtured among family and in family environments. This type of knowledge can include, but is not limited to, kinship ties, notions of care, love, and affection that are unique to the family context.

Questions to consider:

> How can teachers build and sustain learning environments that allow children to share their family histories, stories, and values?

> How can teachers create learning communities that encourage the presence and participation of children's families (e.g., parents, grandparents, aunts, uncles, and adult siblings) in learning in the classroom?

4. **Social capital** emphasizes children's networks, peers, and communities of adult caregivers that can assist with gaining access to information, navigating institutions, understanding unfamiliar situations, and providing opportunities that may not otherwise be available.

Questions to consider:

> How do teachers move beyond deficit accounts of children and their families, and help children recognize the gifts, talents, and strengths of their family and social circles in ways that connect to their family histories, neighborhood assets, community bonds, and personal strengths?

> How do educators engage with children in the world of social media as a learning conduit that is age appropriate, is culturally responsive, and builds on their own ways of knowing?

5. **Navigational capital** refers to children's understanding of and ability to effectively interact in various social institutions, including schools. When children face unsupportive or hostile institutions, their navigational capital is a source of empowerment.

Questions to consider:

> How do teachers help children's families navigate the layers of bureaucracy that often come with enrolling children in new schools or other educational programs?

> How do teachers help families and caregivers understand policies, procedures, jargon, and principles that are endemic in schools (especially if families are not familiar with the language or cultural context)?

6. **Resistant capital** refers to the ability to challenge inequity and disrupt unfair circumstances and situations. Resistant capital emerges from the notion of purposeful oppositional behaviors and the disruption of discrimination in a given context.

Questions to consider:

> How do educators support and understand children who are committed to standing up for peers (or themselves) who they believe are being treated unfairly?

> What learning opportunities can educators provide children to discuss the importance of speaking out against injustice and seeking fairness?

Cultural Capital Among Young African American Children

In many early childhood classrooms, well-intentioned teachers (across the racial and ethnic spectrum) misinterpret students' ways of being, exploring, learning, processing, communicating, and knowing as defiant, disruptive, and deficit oriented. To appropriately recognize and intentionally respond to children's cultural practices, teachers must be open to children's different modes of expression and remain mindful of what those cultural practices might look like in school (Gutiérrez & Rogoff 2003).

I offer three brief snapshots of how cultural capital may manifest itself for some African American learners. (Please keep in mind that cultural capital is dynamic: it changes over time, varies across communities, and is not always manifested in the same ways by all members of a particular group. As such, these are examples to deepen understanding.)

You Are Your Brothers' Keeper

For many African American students, family is of the utmost importance. Some teachers, however, may not understand how integral family ties and fictive kinship bonds are to many young learners' everyday lives. Yosso's (2005) concept of familial capital helps clarify the way some children's experiences in communal environments result in knowledge that helps them form dynamic connections with family and nonfamily members. Consider the following kindergarten scenario:

> **Teacher:** Children, it is time to go to recess. Everyone except Raymond may go outside, because I need to talk to him about his behavior this morning. (*Classroom aide takes children outside, except Raymond; Edward, another student, hangs back.*) Edward, you may go outside; I only need to talk to Raymond.
>
> **Edward:** I'll wait for Raymond.
>
> **Teacher:** Why?
>
> **Edward:** That's my cousin, and I just want to make sure he is okay.
>
> **Teacher:** I didn't know you guys were related. Is that true, Raymond?

Raymond: Uh, yeah . . . we're cousins.

Teacher: I don't think so. How are you related?

Raymond: My mother and Edward's mother are best friends, and we are always at each other's house. So, my mama said we all have to take care of each other. That's why Edward is here, because he knows I might get in trouble, and he wants to make sure I'm okay.

This scenario speaks to the important ties between family, care, and responsibility among many African American children. The type of familial capital shown here reflects a connectedness, even though there are no bloodlines or marriage bonds. *Fictive kinship* (as researchers have labeled this concept) is big in African American culture. It is not uncommon for children to claim as siblings, cousins, aunts, and uncles people with whom there are no lineages, but there are family connections. Moreover, the idea of looking out for a family member is tied to the belief that many African American parents and caregivers stress—you look out for your family. The notion that you are your brothers' keeper has great relevance in the African American community, and many young learners take the responsibility to heart.

Questions to consider:

> How might teachers recognize fictive kinship bonds as legitimate forms of connection among children?

> Are there similar concepts in other cultures, such as the Asian emphasis on the group over the individual, that could be explored in a class project to deepen children's cultural understanding?

> How can teachers acquire a better understanding of family, home, and community practices that inform children's notions of connectedness?

> Should meetings and events that are typically intended for parents be expanded to welcome a broader group of family members and caregivers?

> Could fictive kinship become a model for increasing connectedness and shared responsibility across the entire school community?

Directives Disguised as Questions

Another area where African American cultural capital is typically displayed is language. The following dialogue from a prekindergarten class demonstrates how linguistic practices can manifest themselves for many young African American learners.

Teacher: I would like everyone to come and sit down on the carpet for story time. (*All the children come to the rug except Vincent, who remains at a table.*) Vincent, would you like to come join us for story time?

Vincent: No. I don't want to join.

Teacher: Well, I would like you to join us when you are ready.

Vincent: But I don't wanna join you.

Teacher: We are going to sit on the carpet and begin story time. And when you're ready to join us, please do so.

Vincent: I'm not gonna come over there and join you, because you didn't say that I had to. You just asked me if I wanted to come over, and I don't want to.

In this situation, there is a need to recognize the complexity, nuances, and particulars in language and the role that directives—as opposed to questions—can play in communication. Vincent has locked in on his teacher's *asking him* if he would like to join the circle for story time. Perhaps in Vincent's mind, this request is not a directive but merely a suggestion or preference. Vincent might have reacted differently to a polite form of direct communication, such as "Vincent, you *need* to come sit down on the carpet for story time." Vincent might have understood that participating in story time was not a choice but the teacher's expectation.

Much has been written about the variations, depth, and complexity in African American English vernacular. It is important to note that many African American educators are viewed as being too harsh or stern in their approaches with young learners. Often lost in such assertions is the cultural nuance that, for many African American educators, their approach is serious—not harsh—and conveys deep caring rooted in a request for immediate action. In some of my earlier research, I heard many African American teachers say that they did not have issues of defiance or disrespect from young learners because their students understood the serious tone, tenor, and directness of such firm language (Howard 2010).

Questions to consider:

› How can teachers recognize the subtle messages embedded in their language, phrases, and sayings that can empower or exclude African American (and other non-White) learners?

   • Are there adults of color in your workplace with whom you can discuss language meaning and differences in linguistic cultural capital?

› How do we help students maintain their cultural ways of communicating while also learning and using other forms of discourse, including other cultures' English vernacular and academic English?

› How can teachers and administrators become more sensitive to children's different language experiences and thus to differing linguistic cultural capital?

   • Could a series of workshops with community members on language and culture help staff learn to recognize when a child does not understand a request, directive, or lesson due to cultural differences?

In reading this article, I was struck by Tyrone Howard's assertion that "it is vital for early childhood educators to develop a firm grasp of how students' cultural capital influences the ways students think, speak, process, and make meaning of school situations and circumstances." This statement brought to mind a teacher preparation program I attended in the late '60s, where we were specifically trained and expected to become teacher ethnographers.

The concept of teacher as ethnographer has its roots in the critical pedagogy movement. For more than five decades, this movement has claimed that the key to a successful multicultural classroom is a teacher who engages in self-reflection while getting to know children as individuals whose cultural capital emanates from the context of their social, cultural, political, and economic circumstances (Freire 1968; Gay & Kirkland 2003; hooks 1989).

Ethnographers can take two different perspectives: outsider or insider. When taking the outsider perspective (which is referred to as *etic*), the ethnographer seeks to be an impartial observer; when taking the insider perspective (which is referred to as *emic*), the ethnographer seeks to understand the meaning and beliefs behind local customs. The teacher-training program that I participated in took the insider approach, including the expectation that teachers would live in the communities where they taught.

An overarching goal of the teacher-training program was to develop a positive view of the rich cultural capital and individual agency that children of color, including those from under-resourced communities, bring to the teaching and learning enterprise. Subsumed in this goal was the belief that teachers' knowledge of self (their own cultural capital) would enable them to invest themselves affectively and effectively in efforts to improve children's achievement.

Investment of self refers to teaching in a way that ensures that high-quality learning experiences occur on a daily basis. Investment of self refers to focusing on developing caring relationships with children, modeling enthusiasm and persistence, and exhibiting special care in personal interactions with each child (Sutherland, Lee, & Trapp-Dukes 1989).

The preparation program's conceptual framework regarding teacher as ethnographer was organized around four essential questions:

1. How do race, class, and gender intersect to create oppressive conditions in society?

2. How do schools serve to reproduce social inequality?

3. How can teachers and students resist oppression?

4. How can teachers and students improve students' social and academic trajectories?

Fast-forward to 2018. It is sad but not surprising that these same questions from the late '60s still have agency. And yet, there is reason for hope. Substantial progress has been made in understanding the causes of achievement gaps and the most effective means of addressing them. For young children of color, the achievement gap is real; it starts early, it is persistent, and it is reversible.

As the national debate rages on regarding the knowledge, skills, and dispositions of an excellent early childhood professional, perhaps it would be worthwhile to explore the notion of teacher as ethnographer: What teacher cultural capital is needed for reducing the achievement gap? What would that look like in the context of a 21st century urban school?

A good starting point would be what Loris Malaguzzi, founder of the Reggio Emilia approach, referred to as the "image of the child" (1994). He stated that the teacher's image of the child is where teaching begins. Therefore, believing in the power of the child as a capable, competent, resourceful learner is the first dimension of the cultural capital that the early childhood

professional should bring to the teaching and learning process. This vision requires the capacity to see a child not by the skin color, gender, disability, surname, zip code, or home language, but rather by the promise and possibilities that reside within each child's hopes, dreams, aspirations, and unrealized potential.

The second dimension of the teacher's cultural capital is the capacity to understand the importance of quality relationships: the ability to establish authentic relationships by taking a personal interest in each of the children and conveying to them that they are valued and respected for their cultural agency and that their experiences outside of the classroom are equally as important as their experiences inside the classroom.

The third dimension of the teacher's cultural capital is the capacity to understand the importance of quality conversations: the ability to engage children in meaningful, reciprocal conversations with an appropriate balance of back-and-forth dialogue that models classroom discourse, deepens concept development, builds vocabulary, and promotes accountable talk (Resnick 1999).

The fourth dimension of the teacher's cultural capital is the capacity to understand the quality of experiences: the ability to design and implement a dynamic, robust learning program that is rich in print and conversations that are intellectually stimulating; and where there is a wide range of hands-on, minds-on learning opportunities that build the knowledge and skills that lead to success in school and in life.

The concept of teacher as ethnographer and the four dimensions of teacher cultural capital could serve as key strategies toward improving the social and academic outcomes for children of color. They could also serve as a point of reference as we consider options for developing 21st century early childhood professionals.

(From Sykes 2018)

Resisting for a Reason

In a second grade classroom, the teacher reprimands a student for talking when students were supposed to be listening to the teacher. The reprimanded student explains to her teacher that she was not talking, but that her classmate asked her a question and she was merely responding to the question. When the teacher does not acknowledge the student's explanation, the student becomes angry and frustrated because she has to turn her behavior card from green to yellow. (In this classroom, like many others, there is a behavior management system based on color-coded cards: green = good, yellow = on notice, and red = unacceptable behavior warranting intervention.) Returning to her seat, the young girl refuses to work, and her classmate who asked the question also refuses to work. The girls have seemingly made an unspoken pact as a form of resistance to their teacher, whom they believe has not acknowledged the student's legitimate reason for talking.

Again, Yosso (2005) refers to resistant capital as having its foundations in the experiences of communities of color in securing equal rights and collective freedom. It should be noted that in the face of injustice or in unfair circumstances or situations, resistance can manifest itself even in young learners. This historical legacy of resistance leaves students of color particularly well positioned to leverage their actions as forms of protest, opposition, and what could be interpreted as outright defiance.

Questions to consider:

> How do teachers support students who are committed to fairness in teaching and learning opportunities?

> How do teachers see student resistance as a sign of strength and resilience rather than defiance and deviance?

> How can teachers reflect on their practice to make sure their cultural ways of communicating and evaluating are not putting certain students at a learning disadvantage?

Conclusion

Culture will continue to matter for all learners, but it is frequently misunderstood or ignored where children of color are concerned. Early childhood educators must recognize that all children come to school with culturally rooted knowledge and with dynamic and complex ways of communicating and learning. When each child's cultural capital is understood, learning can be enhanced by instruction that honors these cultural practices and respectfully teaches new practices rooted in other cultures.

It is important for educators not to place the onus for cultural adaptation solely on young learners but on themselves as well. Educators must create cultural bridges that allow both teacher and learner to adopt new ways of learning and understanding. While this responsibility should not rest solely on one side (teacher or student), there is an expectation for teachers, as trained, mature professionals, to take the larger share of responsibility and adapt their understanding to young learners' cultural mores. It is not only professionally appropriate, in many ways it is ethically just. It is vital to some of our most vulnerable student populations, and it is critical to creating democratic and equitable learning opportunities for all children.

Reflection Questions

1. How do you make sure that all of your students see themselves reflected in the curriculum?

2. What steps do you take to aid and support children who are in the ethnic and racial minority in your classroom?

3. In what ways do you reflect on your own personal racial and cultural biases to ensure that they are not informing your practices?

4. What strategies and resources can you use in your classroom to help children appreciate racial, cultural, and ethnic diversity?

5. How do you address your students when issues related to racial differences come up, either in the classroom or the wider community?

References

Artiles, A.J., E.B. Kozleski, S.C. Trent, D. Osher, & A. Ortiz. 2010. "Justifying and Explaining Disproportionality, 1968–2008: A Critique of Underlying Views of Culture." *Exceptional Children* 76 (3): 279–99.

Banks, J.A. 2015. *Cultural Diversity and Education: Foundations, Curriculum, and Teaching.* 6th ed. Boston: Routledge.

Bishop, R.S. 2007. *Free Within Ourselves: The Development of African American Children's Literature.* Portsmouth, NH: Heinemann.

Bloom, B.S., A. Davis, & R. Hess. 1965. *Compensatory Education for Cultural Deprivation.* New York: Holt, Rinehart & Winston.

Boykin, A.W. 1986. "The Triple Quandary and the Schooling of Afro-American Children." Chap. 3 in *The School Achievement of Minority Children: New Perspectives,* ed. U. Neisser, 57–92. Hillsdale, NJ: Erlbaum.

Erickson, F. 2012. "Culture and Education." In *Encyclopedia of Diversity in Education,* Vol. 1, ed. J.A. Banks, 559–68. Thousand Oaks, CA: Sage.

Freire, P. 1968. *Pedagogy of the Oppressed.* New York: Seabury.

Gay, G. 2010. *Culturally Responsive Teaching: Theory, Research, and Practice.* 2nd ed. Multicultural Education Series. New York: Teachers College Press.

Gay, G., & K. Kirkland. 2003. "Developing Cultural Critical Consciousness and Self-Reflection in Preservice Teacher Education." *Theory Into Practice* 42 (3): 181–87.

Gilliam, W.S., A.N. Maupin, C.R. Reyes, M. Accavitti, & F. Shic. 2016. "Do Early Educators' Implicit Biases Regarding Sex and Race Relate to Behavior Expectations and Recommendations of Preschool Expulsions and Suspensions?" Research Study Brief. New Haven, CT: Yale Child Study Center. https://medicine.yale .edu/childstudy/zigler/publications/Preschool%20Implicit%20Bias%20Policy%20Brief_final_9_26 _276766_5379_v1.pdf.

Gutiérrez, K.D., & B. Rogoff. 2003. "Cultural Ways of Learning: Individual Traits or Repertoires of Practice." *Educational Researcher* 32 (5): 19–25.

Harry, B., & J.K. Klingner. 2014. *Why Are So Many Minority Students in Special Education? Understanding Race and Disability in Schools.* 2nd ed. New York: Teachers College Press.

hooks, b. 1989. *Talking Back: Thinking Feminist, Thinking Black.* Toronto: Between the Lines.

Howard, T.C. 2010. *Why Race and Culture Matter in Schools: Closing the Achievement Gap in America's Classrooms.* New York: Teachers College Press.

Ladson-Billings. G. 1995. "Toward a Theory of Culturally Relevant Pedagogy." *American Educational Research Journal* 32 (3): 465–91.

Malaguzzi, L. 1994. "Your Image of the Child: Where Teaching Begins." Trans. and adapted by B. Rankin, L. Morrow, & L. Gandini. From a seminar in Reggio Emilia, Italy, June 1993. www.reggioalliance.org /downloads/malaguzzi:ccie:1994.pdf.

Milner IV, H.R. 2010. *Start Where You Are, but Don't Stay There: Understanding Diversity, Opportunity Gaps, and Teaching in Today's Classrooms.* Cambridge, MA: Harvard Education Press.

Moynihan, D.P. 1965. "The Negro Family: The Case for National Action." US Department of Labor. Washington, DC: Government Printing Office. www.dol.gov/general/aboutdol/history/webid-moynihan.

Nasir, N.S. 2011. *Racialized Identities: Race and Achievement Among African American Youth.* Palo Alto, CA: Stanford University Press.

NCES (US Department of Education, National Center for Education Statistics). 2017. *The Condition of Education 2017.* Report NCES 2017-144. www.nces.ed.gov/pubs2017/2017144.pdf.

OCR (US Department of Education, Office for Civil Rights). 2014. "Civil Rights Data Collection—Data Snapshot: School Discipline." Issue Brief No. 1. https://ocrdata.ed.gov/downloads/crdc-school-discipline -snapshot.pdf.

Resnick, L.B. 1999. "Making America Smarter: A Century's Assumptions About Innate Ability Give Way to a Belief in the Power of Effort." Commentary. *Education Week*, June 16, 38–40.

Skiba, R.J., C.-G. Chung, M. Trachok, T. Baker, A. Sheya, & R. Hughes. 2015. "Where Should We Intervene? Contributions of Behavior, Student, and School Characteristics to Out-of-School Suspension." Chap. 9 in *Closing the School Discipline Gap: Research for Policymakers*, ed. D.J. Losen, 132–46. New York: Teachers College Press.

Sutherland, I.R., M.W. Lee, & R. Trapp-Dukes. 1989. "Teachers' Social Capital: Giving of Oneself." *Early Child Development and Care* 53 (1): 29–35.

Sykes, M. 2018. "A Reason for Hope: Building Teachers' Cultural Capital." *Young Children* 73 (2): 30–31.

Yosso, T.J. 2005. "Whose Culture Has Capital? A Critical Race Theory Discussion of Community Cultural Wealth." *Race, Ethnicity, and Education* 8 (1): 69–91.

About the Author

Tyrone C. Howard is professor of education and associate dean in the Graduate School of Education and Information Studies at the University of California, Los Angeles. His research addresses issues tied to access, equity, race, and culture in schools and communities.

Photographs: pp. 31, 32, 33, 34, 37, 39, 41, 42, © Getty Images

Addressing the African American Achievement Gap

Three Leading Educators Issue a Call to Action

Barbara T. Bowman, James P. Comer, and David J. Johns

Understanding the role of culture in development is important. My first jobs exposed me to people who saw the world differently than I. The more I learned about why they held their beliefs, the more I understood. Today, I ask my [teacher education] students to think about their own cultures and life experiences as the first step in understanding and relating to the children and families they will encounter in the field.

—Barbara T. Bowman

My mother, who had less than two years of formal education, once asked me what I do for a living. I told her I try to incorporate a rich diversity of experiences for kids into educational settings. She said, "Why that's just common sense! They pay you for that?" Common sense, and still it's an uncommon practice among many.

—James P. Comer

Portions of this article are adapted from *Early Learning: A Report for the White House Initiative on Educational Excellence for African Americans*.

We must acknowledge the broader diversity in and of the African American experience and celebrate that all Black children are born geniuses. Black students continue to pursue educational excellence despite the many unnecessary obstacles they face due to constructions and perceptions of race, class, gender, and sexual orientations in America.

—David J. Johns

Early childhood education is an increasingly important aspect of American life, predicting not only later school outcomes but also career and work options, economic stability, health, and social opportunities (Sanders-Phillips et al. 2009). School performance constrains the future opportunities of many African Americans. When matched for social class, the gap in educational achievement between African Americans and other groups is substantial. African American children, on average, score lower on tests and are given lower grades than Asian, White, and Latino students. In adolescence, many of them fail courses and drop out of school. Others progress through school but do not excel; they are less often enrolled in honors courses in high school or accepted into competitive four-year colleges (Stanford CEPA 2018; Valant & Newark 2017).

The achievement gap is a problem not only for African American students and their families and communities; it affects the well-being of the entire country. Researchers have found that "the persistence of the educational achievement gap imposes on the United States the economic equivalent of a permanent national recession" (McKinsey & Company 2009, 6).

Past and present economic and social conditions are at the root of the achievement gap. Societal efforts to overcome the ill effects of prejudice and discrimination for African Americans have not been effective enough; there continue to be inequities in almost every aspect of life, including education (Matthew, Rodrigue, & Reeves 2016; W.K. Kellogg Foundation 2014). At the same time, scientific and technological changes have raised the educational requirements for successful and fulfilling careers, placing an even greater burden on underserved communities and schools. And because social science research has focused primarily on group deficits rather than factors that have stymied progress, it has provided few clues as to how to construct support systems, even where there is a genuine wish to do so.

Only by understanding these factors can teachers develop and implement the strategies needed to move from school failure to school success, increasing opportunities for life success for many more students. Although this article focuses on African American learners, children from other communities of color are often victims of racism and poverty too. Each group has its own unique history with and strategies for coping with oppression, yet they share many of the same challenges and defenses. By understanding the differences and the similarities among groups, teachers can learn the strengths of children and families when designing programs to address their educational and developmental needs.

This article outlines some of the factors that contribute to the achievement gap between African Americans and White Americans and ends with recommendations for educators, administrators, and policymakers to help equalize educational opportunities.

Development and Learning

Like all children, African American children are born with the ability to learn, but require experiences to bring their potential to fruition. Capabilities develop through interactions with people and things that shape the brain circuitry controlling children's physical, social, emotional, and cognitive development. Some aspects of development—like learning language, being sociable, using symbols, and making categories—are propelled by inborn drives to learn. Most children master these tasks at about the same ages and in similar ways.

Other learning is culture specific, such as learning a particular language, creating unique ways to categorize the environment, and interpreting the meanings of events. For example, the vast majority of young children learn language (an inborn drive), but whether they learn Black English or Standard English depends on their experiences in their language communities. So, a child's language acquisition reflects individual and human biological potential, but also it reflects the linguistic characteristics of a particular cultural community.

Children's experiences in the social world of family and community play a critical role in what and how well children learn in school. The importance of warm interpersonal relationships cannot be overstated. Adults are needed to provide consistent physical care, social guidance, intellectual stimulation, and emotional support. Children attach to meaningful caregivers and depend on them for physical and emotional security. They identify with, imitate, and begin to internalize their caregivers' attitudes, values, ways of expressing themselves, and approaches to solving problems; this sets the stage for social, emotional, physical, and cognitive characteristics that in turn affect everything from moral and ethical behavior to manipulative skills and executive functioning.

Children who begin life in safe relationships that are continuously responsive to their evolving needs are most likely to reach out, explore, and learn. This is particularly important for children who live in challenging environments. Further, the most successful learners are born into families that have access to a baseline of resources, including physical security, health care, adequate nutrition, attentive caregiving, and opportunities to learn.

Most African American children have positive adult relationships and achieve their basic developmental potential. That is, at the appropriate ages, they master the complexities of language, process sensory information, manage their bodies, and even use symbols (such as a wooden block to represent a piece of toast). However, some do not have a learning environment that includes opportunities to develop school-related language, knowledge, and skills (such as literacy in Standard English, mathematics, or science). Others, given continued racial exclusion, do not think the work of education will pay off for them. And some are growing up in circumstances that are too stressful for healthy development. These children do not get the extra doses of emotional stability and guidance needed to face the adversity they are exposed to, including adapting to the demands of school.

Racism and Poverty

The interface between racism/classism and attendant economic and social disadvantages is the key to understanding the underachievement of African American children. African Americans have been exposed to generations of legal and illegal measures to deny them basic rights. From slavery to Jim Crow and to today's housing, health care, and voting inequities, the African American community has endured unrelenting racism that begins at an early age (Gershenson & Dee 2017; Gilliam 2014). To believe that these insults have not left a cultural residue—for Whites as well as for African Americans—is to deny what we know about power relationships.

The Burden of Poverty

Without question, poverty places a burden on families, and a large number of African Americans live at an economic level that stresses families physically and mentally, with hunger, mental and physical illness, and despair being frequent corollaries (Matthew, Rodrigue, & Reeves 2016). Poverty among African Americans exceeds that of any other group (USDA 2018). While poverty has declined for White, Hispanic, and Asian families in recent years, it has not for African Americans. In 2015, some 38 percent of Black children lived below the poverty line—a percentage four times greater than that of White or Asian children (Alter 2015). Families struggling to make ends meet are more likely to be stressed and to have less time for their children than those from more economically advantaged groups. In addition, children from poor and also less-poor African American families tend to reside in segregated, underserved neighborhoods, thus concentrating and reinforcing poverty's effects (W.K. Kellogg Foundation 2014).

As a consequence, generations of families and communities have been unable to provide the basic material resources their children require or protect children from the social and emotional stress of racism, poverty, and under-resourced environments. (See "Living with Toxic Stress.") Poverty drains the social and emotional energy of families, making it difficult for adults to respond with constructive guidance to typical childhood behavior, such as aggressiveness or impulsivity. Some families and communities have adapted to the harsh realities they face with aggression. And some children have learned to deal with problems by fighting rather than negotiating or working things out—behavior considered unacceptable in school, especially when teachers and administrators do not understand the roots of the behavior and do not help the children learn new behaviors in a warm, caring, culturally competent way.

Living with Toxic Stress

Exposure to extremes of violence and neglect, inconsistent and unreliable care, and unloving adults can be so stressful for children that their developmental potential is compromised or distorted. The results of such exposure can range from stunted emotional and intellectual development to death. The longer children live in a toxic environment, the more difficult and expensive it is to help them return to more typical developmental and learning trajectories (Shonkoff et al. 2012).

Too many African American children live in toxic environments. Given this, it is a testament to African American families that despite the challenges they face, so many find the resources to help their children avoid the more serious developmental and learning problems. However, early recognition of and support for children being affected by a toxic environment are essential if children are to avoid the pitfalls of failed development and a compromised future; exposure to severe neglect and abuse is increasingly difficult to treat. Timely family counseling and treatment, supportive alternative caregivers (often a grandparent or sitter), understanding teachers, supportive friends and neighbors, and/or therapeutic intervention can play a role in reducing stress and stabilizing children's development.

The Role of Culture and Tradition

Culture is what groups create over time to adapt to their environment; it determines to a large extent how adults interact with children. Throughout the world, as families adapt to different environmental challenges, they develop different childrearing strategies, many of which are misunderstood by those unfamiliar with a community's history. For instance, as a result of transatlantic enslavement, Black people mixed the remnants of their home languages with English to create a dialect, or *patois,* to communicate with one another since they did not share a common language. The remnants continue today as Black English. The public impression, however, which has been used to justify abuse and injustice, is that this adaptive language, this dialect, is "bad" or broken English. Among those with limited knowledge of Black culture and linguistics, Black English is mistakenly assumed to be a product of ignorance rather than a creative form of verbal communication as complex as Standard English (Labov 1972).

Other behaviors that were fashioned to help African Americans cope with the dangers of slavery continue today because life is still perceived as dangerous. For instance, African American children are often criticized for passivity, limited oral responsiveness, and disengagement (Labov 1972). Yet many Black families teach this behavior as the best way for children to be safe in a hostile world. Rather than embracing new experiences outside the safety of family, children are encouraged to attenuate their responsiveness with others to avoid trouble (Calarco 2014; Labov 1972). Even though these strategies tend not to be advantageous in the school environment, they have lingered because they keep children emotionally safe in the segregated society in which most of them live.

The systemic challenges of poverty and racism continue today for African American families and children (W.K. Kellogg Foundation 2014), and families respond in different ways (Duncan, Brooks-Gunn, & Klebanov 1994). Some experience self-doubt and powerlessness, others deny their culture and language to avoid rejection, and still others respond with rage or detachment. While many of these responses may seem nonfunctional, they are designed to protect children from the prejudice and discrimination encountered by most African Americans with appalling frequency.

Unaware of the culturally adaptive reasons for behavior, many people—even many African Americans—are unaware of the strengths that have enabled African American communities to survive and thrive despite deep hardships. Teachers who understand the history of slavery, the restrictions of segregation, and the continued injustices encountered by African Americans can better understand African American children's behavior. In the past, tight-knit family networks and communities of teachers and leaders were better able to support children and buffer the negative messages children received from the larger society. Today, the lack of knowledge about and appreciation for Black culture creates social distance between African Americans and White Americans and is a deterrent to change. The African American culture transmitted from generation to generation needs to be understood as rich and noteworthy, and needs to be used as the entry to new skills and knowledge. By recognizing the meaning and value of children's home knowledge, teachers can use home culture as a foundation from which to extend children's thinking rather than considering it an impediment.

While culture carries with it the past, it also constantly adapts to new conditions and new challenges. As people adapt, they integrate the old with the new, often using the old to help transition to the new. The traditional African American interest in music has led to innovations, such as jazz and rap, and to newer music forms; the traditional physicality in the African American community has led to high performance in athletics; the interest in language is reflected in the contributions Black people have made to the imaginative use of words (slang, for example). Many of the rules and concepts of school overlap with much of what children already know—but often children need teachers and school system leaders to help them see the overlap. For example, many Black children have strong interests in and knowledge about sports and entertainment. They need supportive teachers to help them see how academics are related to these interests and will enhance what they already know. The capabilities developed in homes and communities can be used as springboards for learning in school *if teachers recognize children's strengths* (Adair 2015). Building on strengths, achievement can soar.

Exposure to poverty and prejudice are not uniform across the African American population; not all African Americans are poor or failing in school. Yet disproportionately their achievement and life circumstances are constrained by race and class. Almost every aspect of life at every income level is affected—housing, employment, health care, education, and social acceptance—all of which have long- and short-term implications for school achievement (Pager & Shepherd 2008; Reardon 2015). The systemic challenges of the Black experience continue today for families and children (W.K. Kellogg Foundation 2014). Poverty and racism, past and present, compromise the ability of many poor and minority families—especially African American families—to provide the secure base young children need (Grusky, Varner, & Mattingly 2015). The ultimate solution to the education gap is the elimination of race and class prejudice and oppression. In the meantime, creating an ultra-supportive environment appears to be the best—perhaps the only—chance for children from challenging backgrounds to be successful in school and in life (Robert Wood Johnson Foundation 2016). This means providing supports for families and education for children, and promoting understanding among teachers and administrators.

The Challenges of School

If most African American families typically provide the experiences necessary for healthy growth and development, why do so many African American children have trouble learning in school? One reason is the differing expectations for children between home and school. The skills and knowledge children gain at home and in their communities often do not match schools' demands. Home cultures do not prevent African American children from learning in school, but some home practices are not similar to or synchronous with school culture.

Returning to language, children who learn Black English at home, as opposed to learning Standard English, have a steeper learning curve for school reading and writing because Standard English is very similar to academic English. For Black children, particularly those from families with low income in highly segregated communities, there is more likely to be a poor fit between their language experiences and what schools require. This misalignment becomes a barrier to school learning unless it is addressed early.

Like other children, African American children—even those from families with low income—have information about their immediate environment and learn through their experiences. However, they may not have the same knowledge base as children from other communities, particularly children from more economically advantaged ones. They may not have the academic and social knowledge that teachers expect. They know the names of things, ideas, people, and places that are meaningful to them, but they may not know letter names or how to hold a book or what a farm is or how to count to 20. Because of this, they are often viewed as developmentally delayed or having limited potential to learn. Thus, even though they have achieved developmental milestones, they may begin to fail in school.

African American children who go to school without a sound foundation of school-type information are at a profound disadvantage, making the achievement gap inevitable at school entry—but not insurmountable. For example, children from families with lower income hear fewer words and have smaller vocabularies, on average, than children from more financially advantaged families (Hart & Risley 1995). This disadvantages African American children, since a larger proportion of them are poorer than White children. While a smaller vocabulary may not be a linguistic problem (the children have a language, just not Standard English), it does mean a child is likely to have trouble with listening comprehension in the early grades, especially when teachers read aloud complex texts that use Standard and academic English vocabulary. What starts out as simply a disparity in vocabulary escalates over the elementary grades to difficulty with reading comprehension, on which all later learning depends. Struggling with reading may also become a social challenge, leading to misbehavior and a lack of motivation to try (often fueled by embarrassment at being behind one's peers). Therefore, it is essential to address the vocabulary difference before it morphs into school failure.

Another problem for many African American children is the lack of continuity between the preschool years and the primary grades (Takanishi 2016). Research and school experience have shown the importance of long-term consistency in expectations, high-quality instruction, and social supports if children from low-income homes are to master the challenges of school. In the first several years of their lives, many African American children remain at home or are in child care arrangements in which school prerequisites (e.g., formal literacy and numeracy experiences) and social and emotional support (e.g., responsive teachers) are not a part of daily life.

For children who do not learn Standard English at home and are enduring the stresses of growing up in isolated and/or under-resourced communities, even attending preschool may not be enough. Children may require additional social and academic supports the first four or five years in school if they are to reach their potential. They need meaningful relationships with teachers who believe they can learn, whom they want to please. They need carefully structured curricula that build across grade levels so that children have the prior knowledge necessary to succeed. They also need teachers who coach them in how to get their needs met in school, how to ask for help, and how to accept it. And finally, they need teachers and administrators who communicate well with their families and can help the families be supportive of their children's academic learning.

Educating Our Educators

Essential to narrowing the achievement gap is the education of early childhood educators. Teachers and administrators need preservice preparation and ongoing professional development that enable them to understand that most African American children are not underdeveloped or developmentally delayed. When teachers use effective engagement methods, African American children can achieve the same academic and social development in school as other children. Preparatory institutions and professional development programs must prepare educators to understand the manner in which child development and academic learning are inextricably linked and how they can facilitate learning for children from different backgrounds.

Children with Developmental Delays and Disabilities

Certainly some children have developmental delays or disabilities that may require different teaching strategies because of biological differences (such as having Down syndrome) or because of life experiences (such as living with toxic stress) or both. They need teachers with special skills to recognize and meet their needs. Other children—the vast majority—are typically developing and need a genuine opportunity to learn the foundational skills and knowledge expected by schools. During the preschool years, children need to be assessed for biological and social difficulties, with interventions provided as needed. However, all children—of all abilities—need to be fully engaged so they become enthusiastic learners of their schools' curricula.

Cultural Differences

Teachers also need a better understanding of cultural differences and similarities. Too often, teachers and administrators view the different expressions of development in African

Americans as evidence of intentionally bad and distasteful behavior and/or low academic potential. When African American children demonstrate adaptive behaviors (such as passivity or aggression) that have been successful in the past, teachers and administrators usually spend little time trying to understand the etiology of these behaviors or the systems that cause them. They simply label the children "special needs" or delinquent and exclude them from grade-level curricula.

When teachers—often through little fault of their own—do not understand the reasons for children's behavior, they are likely to lower their expectations for children of color. The children internalize their teachers' evaluations of their potential, thus lowering their own (and often their families') expectations for achievement. Underfunded schools that provide little support or professional guidance for inexperienced teachers and administrators compound the problem.

In the past, informal networks of families and neighbors provided the supports many African American children and families needed. Today, because of increased pressures in homes and neighborhoods, formal organizations (social, educational, political, economic, philanthropic, and community) often must step in. To be more effective, these organizations must rethink how they deliver their services. Depersonalized, rule-governed relationships must give way to intentional connections and meaningful collaboration. The most effective way to bring about and sustain such relationships is through local action in which Black families are meaningfully engaged. Schools in particular play an important role in defusing racism, educating staff, providing social networks (activities), and welcoming families. If the achievement gap is to be closed, schools need to continue their commitment to children from before birth into young adulthood, with regular updates to meet changing social needs.

Conclusion

Acting on research and intervention findings, some of which are presented here, will require embracing new understanding and accepting the discomfort of change. Established economic, political, social, and even structural interests are involved in the status quo. Long-term change will only happen when these systems reflect a culturally appropriate, asset-based understanding of the children and families they serve. It will require educators, administrators, and policymakers who

> Know that today's education is needed for the US economy and the future of American democracy

> Understand the economic, political, and social contexts of families and recognize the complex interactions between all of these and children's learning in school

> Appreciate that education begins before birth and that preschool education is as essential as K–12 for all children at risk for school failure

> Understand that a good education is far more than good test scores (although those are important); physical and mental health, the arts and music, citizenship responsibilities, and empathic relationships are equally important and should be planned for and supported in school

> See the importance of facilitating engagement and learning for children from non-White backgrounds; of integrating a positive racial identity with development; and of understanding teaching and learning as intellectually stimulating and culturally affirming experiences

> Plan for the prevention of challenging behaviors and the promotion of responsible and effective family support to reduce costly generation-to-generation transmission of unrewarding behavior

> Work to foster authentic, reciprocal partnerships between families, children, teachers, and schools, in which the achievement of all students is encouraged and supported at home and at school

> Select curricula and use teaching practices that are developmentally and culturally appropriate and thus are based on children's needs (rather than one size fits all)

> Ensure that all children are given opportunities to develop an identity of excellence and scholarship that counters negative stereotypes

> Recognize cultural differences and set high academic expectations for all children

Reflection Questions

1. After reading this article, identify some reasons why it is possible for healthy, well-developed African American children with supportive families to struggle or fail in school.

2. Can you think of something from your community's history (e.g., a ritual, a story, a belief) that is still important to you today?

3. *Privilege* is a benefit that comes with who you are, not what you do. Can you think of specific situations in which you've benefitted from privilege or times in which others have been privileged over you?

4. Cultures are almost always changing. Talk with older members of your family or community to identify prejudices that have changed over time and those that have persisted.

5. Is your community segregated? Consider education spaces (Are schools composed of people who are mostly one race?), housing (Do African Americans and White Americans live, for the most part, separately from one another?), and social interactions (Do you belong to organizations, clubs, or friend groups that are primarily one race?).

We believe that a program carried out by people and organizations with a deep understanding of the complexities and the collaborations needed to support child development, who recognize the importance of education—both what is taught and how it is taught—and who focus resources to support family functioning will help close the achievement gap, benefiting our children, families, economy, and democracy.

References

Adair, J.K. 2015. *The Impact of Discrimination on the Early Schooling Experiences of Children from Immigrant Families.* Report. Migration Policy Institute. www.migrationpolicy.org/research/impact-discrimination-early-schooling-experiences-children-immigrant-families.

Alter, C. 2015. "Black Children Still Most Likely to Live in Poverty, Study Says." *Time*, July 14. www.time.com/3955671/black-children-poverty-study.

Calarco, J.M. 2014. "Coached for the Classroom: Parents' Cultural Transmission and Children's Reproduction of Educational Inequalities." *American Sociological Review* 79 (5): 1015–37.

Duncan, G.J., J. Brooks-Gunn, & P.K. Klebanov. 1994. "Economic Deprivation and Early Childhood Development." *Child Development* 65 (2): 296–318.

Gershenson, S., & T.S. Dee. 2017. "The Insidiousness of Unconscious Bias in Schools." *Brown Center Chalkboard* (blog), March 20. Brookings. www.brookings.edu/blog/brown-center-chalkboard/2017/03/20/the-insidiousness-of-unconscious-bias-in-schools.

Gilliam, W.S. 2014. "What Could Make Less Sense than Expelling a Preschooler?" *Psychology Benefits Society* (blog), December 13. American Psychological Association. https://psychologybenefits.org/2014/12/13/preschool-expulsions.

Grusky, D., C. Varner, & M. Mattingly, eds. 2015. "State of the States: The Poverty and Inequality Report." *Pathways: A Magazine on Poverty, Inequality, and Social Policy*. Special issue. The Stanford Center on Poverty and Inequality. http://inequality.stanford.edu/sites/default/files/SOTU_2015.pdf.

Hart, B., & T.R. Risley. 1995. *Meaningful Differences in the Everyday Experience of Young American Children*. Baltimore, MD: Brookes.

Labov, W. 1972. *Language in the Inner City: Studies in Black English Vernacular*. Conduct and Communication series. Philadelphia: University of Pennsylvania Press.

Matthew, D.B., E. Rodrigue, & R.V. Reeves. 2016. *Time for Justice: Tackling Race Inequalities in Health and Housing*. Report. Washington, DC: Brookings. www.brookings.edu/research/time-for-justice-tackling-race -inequalities-in-health-and-housing.

McKinsey & Company. 2009. *The Economic Impact of the Achievement Gap in America's Schools: Summary of Findings*. Report. http://dropoutprevention.org/wp-content/uploads/2015/07/ACHIEVEMENT_GAP _REPORT_20090512.pdf.

Pager, D., & H. Shepherd. 2008. "The Sociology of Discrimination: Racial Discrimination in Employment, Housing, Credit, and Consumer Markets." *Annual Review of Sociology* 34: 181–209. www.ncbi.nlm.nih.gov /pmc/articles/PMC2915460.

Reardon, S.F. 2015. "School Segregation and Racial Academic Achievement Gaps." CEPA (Stanford Center for Education Policy Analysis) Working Paper No. 15-12. https://cepa.stanford.edu/sites/default/files/wp15 -12v201510.pdf.

Robert Wood Johnson Foundation. 2016. "Can Early Childhood Interventions Improve Health and Well-Being?" *Health Policy Snapshot Series*. www.rwjf.org/en/library/research/2016/03/can-early-childhood -interventions-improve-life-outcomes-.html.

Sanders-Phillips, K., B. Settles-Reaves, D. Walker, &, J. Brownlow. 2009. "Social Inequality and Racial Discrimination: Risk Factors for Health Disparities in Children of Color." *Pediatrics* 124 (Supplement 3): S176–86. http://pediatrics.aappublications.org/content/124/Supplement_3/S176.

Shonkoff, J.P., A.S. Garner, American Academy of Pediatrics (AAP) Committee on Psychosocial Aspects of Child and Family Health, AAP Committee on Early Childhood, Adoption, and Dependent Care, AAP Section on Developmental and Behavioral Pediatrics, B.S. Siegel, M.I. Dobbins, M.F. Earls, A.S. Garner, L. McGuinn, J. Pascoe, & D.L. Wood. 2012. "The Lifelong Effects of Early Childhood Adversity and Toxic Stress." Technical report. *Pediatrics* 129 (1): e232–46.

Stanford CEPA. 2018. "Racial and Ethnic Achievement Gaps." The Educational Opportunity Monitoring Project. Accessed May 1. http://cepa.stanford.edu/educational-opportunity-monitoring-project/achievement-gaps /race.

Takanishi, R. 2016. *First Things First! Creating the New American Primary School*. New York: Teachers College Press.

USDA (US Department of Agriculture). 2018. "Poverty Demographics." Rural Poverty and Well-Being. Last modified April 18. www.ers.usda.gov/topics/rural-economy-population/rural-poverty-well-being.

Valant, J., & D. Newark. 2017. "Race, Class, and Americans' Perspectives of Achievement Gaps." *Brown Center Chalkboard* (blog), January 16. Brookings. www.brookings.edu/blog/brown-centerchalkboard/2017/01/16 /race-class-and-americans-perspectives-of-achievement-gaps.

W.K. Kellogg Foundation. 2014. "New Poll Reveals Challenges and Opportunities Facing African American Families." News and Media, April 1. www.wkkf.org/news-and-media/article/2014/04/new-poll-reveals -challenges-and-opportunities-facing-african-american-families.

About the Authors

Barbara T. Bowman is the Irving B. Harris Professor at Erikson Institute. She was chief officer for early childhood education at the Chicago Public Schools (2004–2012) and a consultant to the US Department of Education (2009), and she served on the White House Initiative on Educational Excellence for African Americans (2014–2016).

James P. Comer, MD, MPH, is the Maurice Falk Professor of Child Psychiatry at the Yale University Child Study Center. In 1968, he founded the Comer School Development Program, which promotes the collaboration of families, educators, and community to improve social, emotional, and academic outcomes for children.

David J. Johns is the executive director of the National Black Justice Coalition in Washington, DC, and is a PhD student at Teachers College, Columbia University. David previously served as the executive director of the White House Initiative on Educational Excellence for African Americans and was appointed to the position by President Barack H. Obama.

Photographs: pp. 45, 46, 47, 50, 52, © Getty Images

Voices of Immigrant Families in Early Childhood Settings

Jennifer Keys Adair and Alejandra Barraza

When immigrant families enroll their children in US early education programs, it is often with a mix of hope and apprehension. Many immigrant families are grateful for and feel optimistic about the education their children will receive. But some worry that their children's teachers won't understand all aspects of their culture or will be unable to advocate for their children in the classroom. In the United States, as in other countries, these concerns can be connected to disparaging and discriminatory comments and attitudes circulating in the larger society about immigration and immigrants. In addition, some teachers have limited experience with or education about the immigrant communities they serve (Arzubiaga & Adair 2010).

Children Crossing Borders Project

In extensive focus group interviews, more than 100 immigrant families in five US cities, as part of the multisite ethnographic study Children Crossing Borders (CCB), shared their concerns and hopes about the characteristics of their children's teachers. The ideas, strategies, and concerns recorded from the interviews with immigrant families demonstrate that these families, like all families, are important sources of information about their young children and their schooling. They can help teachers understand what it means to be a young immigrant family in the United States.

The CCB research team (which included one of the authors—Jennifer) interviewed families who came from a variety of countries, including Mexico, Iraq, Egypt, Dominican Republic, Sudan, Côte d'Ivoire, and Nigeria (Tobin, Arzubiaga, & Adair 2013). Because it is often difficult to ask families, particularly immigrant families, about sensitive subjects like home–school relationships, immigration, and discrimination, rather than asking a list of interview questions, researchers showed a video of a preschool to get people talking. This research method is called *video-cued multivocal ethnography*, perhaps more commonly known as the Preschool in Three Cultures method developed by Joseph Tobin and colleagues (Tobin, Hsueh, & Karasawa 2009; Tobin, Wu, & Davidson 1989) over the past 30 years.

Teachers as Cultural Beings

Engaging in culturally relevant ways of teaching immigrant children requires teachers to examine their own cultural experiences, beliefs, and values (Derman-Sparks & Ramsey 2011; Souto-Manning 2013a) and to acknowledge the ways that their experiences and identities shape their teaching. This is key, as many teachers tend to regard their own schooling aculturally, as "just the way it is." They may thus teach the way they were taught—ethnocentrically—regarding their own schooling experience as the norm against which all others must be scaled and rated (Goodwin & Genor 2008; Souto-Manning 2010), without regard for the cultural nature of teaching and learning.

Given that early childhood teachers in the United States are predominantly White, middle class, monolingual women (Aud, Fox, & KewalRamani 2010; Souto-Manning & Cheruvu 2016), and may have limited experience with multilingual communities of color, many may see diversities in negative terms, believing in dangerous stereotypes—for example, that homeless people are lazy, that African American English is wrong or broken English, or that speaking languages other than English will disadvantage children academically (Derman-Sparks & Ramsey 2011; Goodwin & Genor 2008). These views are at least partly due to the fact that teacher education and developmental psychology have not historically positioned culture as a central aspect of early childhood teacher preparation or of child development (Souto-Manning & Martell 2016). Knowledge, practices, interactions, and individuals are not culture-free (Goodwin & Genor 2008; Souto-Manning 2013a), yet they tend to be seen as such in many early childhood education settings (Goodwin, Cheruvu & Genishi 2008; New & Mallory 1994).

While it is important for teachers to learn about children's experiences and cultural practices, before doing so, it is imperative that they first analyze their own identities, coming to see themselves as cultural beings (Goodwin & Genor 2008; Nieto 2010; Souto-Manning 2013a). Culturally relevant teachers start by acknowledging the cultural knowledge and practices that shape their approaches to teaching all children (Ladson-Billings 1995; Souto-Manning & Martell 2016), including those from immigrant families. This is not an easy task, nor is it a practice that can be fully described in this article. Yet teachers need to ask themselves, "Who am I as a cultural being?"

If teachers believe that they have grown up in a cultural vacuum and have no culture, it is perhaps an indication of the privileges associated with their cultural backgrounds and practices (Derman-Sparks & Ramsey 2011). Some examples of privileged categories (which are often perceived by many as normal) include White, dominant American English speaker, and heterosexual (Cahnmann-Taylor & Souto-Manning 2010).

As part of the CCB study, immigrant families and preschool teachers in five cities (Nuevo Campo and Phoenix, Arizona; Nashville, Tennessee; Riverdale, Iowa; and New York City) watched a 20-minute film showing a typical day in an NAEYC-accredited preschool in Phoenix. (Nuevo Campo and Riverdale are fictitious names to protect the privacy of participants from these small communities.) The program serves many children of immigrants, mostly from Spanish-speaking families. The film includes typical preschool scenes that most US preschool teachers would recognize, such as children arguing over a dress in the dramatic play area and clapping along with a song during group time. Also shown in the film are high-quality (and perhaps less often seen) preschool classroom features, such as Spanish-speaking teachers and signage in Spanish and English throughout the classroom. In the text that follows, we focus on how the immigrant families in the CCB study reacted to the preschool practices they saw in the filmed classroom, telling us what they liked and didn't like, what was different from their own early childhood experiences, and whether the program looked like their children's classrooms.

Seeing themselves as cultural beings is essential for all educators, so they can recognize that the many cultural resources children have in their homes and communities are worthy, and not merely stepping stones that children can leave behind once they master the knowledge and practices to be learned in school (Souto-Manning 2010, 2013a). Moving outside their cultural comfort zone is necessary in order for educators "to view children, their families, and members of their communities as our most important teachers" (Long et al. 2008, 253) and to more fully understand the experiences of children from immigrant families.

Engaging in home visits and in the mapping of community resources can be valuable ways for teachers to learn about children's families, better understanding the cultural practices shaping their development and learning. Teachers can learn from family and community interactions, document their cultural practices, and bring them into the classroom as curricula and through teaching strategies.

Engaging in critical inquiry encourages teachers, children, and family members to collaboratively learn about their communities, and involves teachers and children who engage in "grand conversations" (Eeds & Wells 1989, 1) in both wondering and information-seeking forms of dialogue (Lindfors 1999).

From the students' interests, inquiry expands and grows to address and approach a variety of content areas. Inquiry brings together content areas in interdisciplinary and authentic ways through students' questions and interests. It brings together a variety of backgrounds and resources—some of which are typically included in the traditional classroom, and others that are not. Inquiry is a space where the personal and academic converge and craft an interdisciplinary and culturally relevant curriculum. (Souto-Manning 2013a, 42)

Through critical inquiry, learners can collectively uncover the social and cultural nature of knowledge. Critical inquiry can come to life as equity pedagogy, which encompasses culturally relevant practices, thus restructuring the classroom environment in more equitable and inclusive ways. Such restructuring necessitates young children becoming curriculum codesigners. After all, they are the full participants in their families' and communities' cultural practices—practices teachers may have observed but not experienced (Souto-Manning 2010).

(From Souto-Manning 2013b)

Immigrant Families' Suggestions for Early Childhood Educators

The diverse groups of immigrant families who watched and responded to the film had different ideas about children's learning, play, appropriate family–child–teacher interactions, and child guidance, but there were some commonalities among the families' views of teacher qualities. The following are seven suggestions offered by numerous immigrant families from multiple cultural, linguistic, and ethnic groups for teachers who work with young children of immigrants.

1. Be Affectionate with Children

One scene in the video caught the attention of most of the immigrant families:

> Michael, barely 4 years old, holds back sobs as he enters the classroom. While his mother signs him in, Michael clings to her leg. He sniffles, looking up periodically. When his mother takes him over to Liliana, the teacher, Michael lets out a wail. After the mother leaves, Liliana holds the sobbing child, cuddling him, talking softly to him, and congratulating him when he calms down.

When the families watched this scene, many voiced sympathy for Michael and his mother. They also praised Liliana for the way she comforted the child and helped him feel better. Juana, a mother from Mexico, explained,

> I liked the way the teacher hugged the little boy when he started crying after his mom left. She tried to comfort him right away. It is important for the teacher to try to make the student feel safe.

Juana, like many family members, used words like *hug, comfort, patience,* and *feeling safe* to describe how teachers should treat children in the classroom. Although families in the study had a lot to say about learning, these were typically their first responses, rather than comments about curriculum or the classroom environment.

Immigrant families said that when children have separation anxiety or cry, it is important for teachers to be affectionate with them. "Like a mom," said a mother in one of the New York City preschools. Explained a mother in Riverdale, "Affection makes the children feel wanted and welcomed. They are more apt to tell you if something is wrong if you are close to them." Teachers can mirror how families show affection to their children and ask families how best to comfort their children when they are sad, confused, frustrated, or tired. Immigrant families voiced deep concern that their children might be suffering without the teacher noticing or understanding why. Teachers can hug children to demonstrate that they are safe and cared for. When families saw their own child's teacher hug children in the classroom, families reported that this affection was a signal to them that their children would be watched over carefully.

2. Be Patient with Children

Families worried about whether teachers were patient with young children of immigrants. They believed that language barriers, shyness, and new environments might prevent children from learning things as quickly as they might otherwise. During one interview in Nuevo Campo, when families were asked what advice they would give to teachers who work with young children of immigrants—especially to teachers who are not immigrants or don't speak the same language—this is what they said:

> **Consuela:** First of all, [teachers] should be very patient with [immigrant children] because [the children] don't know the language. Because a child is very intelligent.

> **Inéz:** To be patient with them, the ones arriving from Mexico. To speak some Spanish . . .

> **Consuela:** Because it's the same as if you didn't know Spanish and you were going to Mexico. You would feel bad, wouldn't you, that they didn't understand you?

> **Elena:** Not treating [children] bad because they are Mexicans.

Families in our discussions shared experiences in grocery stores, banks, doctors' offices, and at the front desk of the school, where they felt ignored or hurried along because they didn't speak English or were from another country. Muslim immigrant families in Phoenix shared stories of their children being taunted by classmates and community members after the events of September 11. Riverdale families shared stories of missing out on important curriculum and program decisions for their children because they did not receive notices or could not read them in English. Patience from preschool teachers is especially important to immigrant families, many of whom may experience a society that is impatient with them.

Like Consuela, Elena, and Inéz, many families in our study believe in their children's ability to learn. But they are also realistic about their learning in English—it may take longer because English is often a new language for children of immigrants. It is important for teachers to willingly go over concepts, books, materials, and instructions multiple times and in a calm way. Immigrant families spoke positively about teachers who work with children over and over and who "don't give up on children." Families thought it was important to help young children of immigrants learn English in a kind way, without pushing them too hard or making them feel that they are far behind children whose home language is English.

3. Be Respectful with Families

When teachers asked immigrant families watching the film of the Phoenix preschool their opinions about the teaching practices or the learning environment, the families found it difficult to be critical of the teacher. It seemed much easier to point out the *practices* they liked and didn't like. One father explained that Latino families have huge respect for teachers and often address them as *maestra* rather than by name. Too often, however, this respect is not reciprocal, and schools take advantage of this respect and ignore the cultural wealth of Latino families (Yosso 2006).

At the preschools in Riverdale and Nashville, where families and teachers rarely saw one another and operated in different cultural communities, preschool teachers made some inaccurate assumptions about immigrant families' feelings regarding their children's education. For example, in Riverdale, preschool teachers reported that families were appreciative of their children's education and seemed to be generally accepting of what happened at school. The families told us they were grateful for their children's education but had questions about education issues they were hesitant to raise with the teachers or staff. Many families were concerned about their ability to help with schoolwork or worried about whether their children would be ready for kindergarten or would stop speaking Spanish because there were no Spanish-speaking teachers.

In Iowa, Sudanese families spoke about the cultural barriers between themselves and the school. One mother, Fazilah, described an incident with her young daughter and the school's principal. Her daughter had explained that she was born in Africa and the principal corrected her and said she was born in the United States. Her daughter was upset, so Fazilah met with the principal to explain how her daughter views her complicated identity.

Suggestions

Schools and teachers that are respectful, according to immigrant families in the study, work hard to support families in their role as their children's first teachers. This means asking families about their children, having translators at family–teacher conferences, translating newsletters into home languages, and asking for input on the optimal early learning environments for their children. To establish respect for families' cultures and experiences, teachers might ask families whether the education they see in the classroom is similar to or different from what they remember in their home country. Ask whether there is anything they would like to see in the classroom or whether something seems to be missing. If families are able to visit the classroom, teachers can point out everyday conflicts or occurrences and ask for input about how such incidents would be handled at home.

If a family remains relatively quiet during conferences and visits, show them samples of their child's work to illustrate the child's progress. An interesting video clip or photograph can show how their child acts in a social situation or works intently with different materials. Families in the study had a lot to say when they watched their own children on camera. Many enjoyed learning more about what happens in school during the day. One of the teachers in the study commented that after families watched the film, they had many comments and questions about classroom routines and curriculum.

4. Use or Learn Words in the Home Language

Families in the study wanted their children to have bilingual teachers who could advocate for their children at school and within the larger community. They felt that monolingual teachers who attempted to speak some of their home language demonstrated support for bilingual families and respect for the immigrant community. Families appreciated teachers who learned everyday phrases like "Hello, how are you?," "Thank you," and "Your child did well today."

Teachers who speak English and the same language as the immigrant families are invaluable, not just for their language skills but often for their insight into how difficult it can be to learn a new language and to understand new cultural rules. Families felt that teachers who could speak the child's home language could use it to advocate for their child, intervene on the child's behalf, and communicate directly with families. In Phoenix, one father wondered how a teacher could know a child was being teased or left out if she didn't understand the child's language. Families told us that when their children had to translate for them at school conferences or meetings with teachers, it damaged the family–teacher relationship because it made them feel more an immigrant and less a parent. Immigrant families in all five cities agreed that for families to participate in their children's educational experience, it is important and necessary for the school to provide translators.

Suggestions

Teachers can advocate for their schools to be responsible for appropriate translation, and they can actively seek volunteers and mentors from the immigrant communities of the families they serve. Early childhood teachers in New York organized a family group so that immigrant families from previous years, whose children had already left the preschool for elementary school, could mentor new families at the preschool.

Teachers who do not speak the family's language can learn words and phrases from the children in their classroom, and use games and learning center activities that teach or support words in the languages of the communities served in the classroom (Marinak, Strickland, & Keat 2010). Such learning is not going to result in teachers' fluency, but it demonstrates support to families. Before a translator joins a conference or visit, immigrant families and preschool teachers can try to communicate directly. Attempts by families and teachers to learn some of each other's language is a step toward equalizing the relationship.

5. Approach Families as Experts on Their Children

Immigrant families often remarked that preschool teachers explained a lot about teaching strategies to them but rarely asked questions about their child. In New York City, immigrant families from Nigeria and Côte d'Ivoire pointed out that the teachers spent most of the home visit explaining academic instruction and what their responsibility was as families. Immigrant families in Riverdale and Phoenix agreed. Even families who really liked their child's teacher were frustrated when the teacher explained school issues during meetings, rather than answering their questions or listening and responding to their concerns.

Suggestions

Immigrant families, like most families, may be hesitant at first to comment on teaching practices but are usually quick to share stories about their own children. During home visits and conferences, take time to ask the families about their children to validate their role as experts about their children. Ask them about their children's likes and dislikes, what they enjoy learning, how they learn best, what tricks they use for helping the children stay on task, and what they would do in certain situations and why. Questions are more effective if they are open ended. Teachers do have routines, curriculum, and organizational issues to explain to families, but asking questions and treating families as experts provides avenues for families to be more involved in their children's education and for teachers to gain helpful insight into how the children in their classrooms learn.

6. Learn About Children Before School Begins

Some immigrant families in the study suggested that teachers get to know children before they enter the classroom. To do this, teachers have to rely on the expertise of the families, rather than on their own observations. Josephina wished that she could have explained her daughter's shyness to the teacher before the school year began.

> My child is too shy . . . she barely talks. I want to tell the teacher that she is not sick . . . it doesn't mean that she doesn't want to play with other children, but she has been like that all the time.

Josephina felt that if the teachers had known this beforehand, they would have watched out for her daughter more effectively on the playground and in the classroom. Perhaps, Josephina thought, they would have been more understanding of certain behaviors and helped her child socialize with different groups of children. She felt that in early educational settings it was important to know the *individuo* (individual), or the whole child.

Suggestions

It is important for teachers to welcome and encourage immigrant families to share their knowledge about their children. Families can ask for a translator when communication is a struggle, especially to share their thoughts and ideas about their children before or at the beginning of the school year. Honest curiosity from teachers about children coming into the classroom enables families to share their knowledge about their children and establish a relationship with the school.

Gathering information about each child in a classroom could involve home visits, family questionnaires, informational school meetings, family–teacher conferences before school begins, family visits or volunteer time to help with specific projects, meeting with new families at the end of the previous school year, and asking families to tell you about some of their children's likes and dislikes on the first day of school. These ideas support many recent articles in *Young Children* that focus on asking questions and getting expertise on preschool-age children from their families (see Kersey & Masterson 2009; Nagel & Wells 2009).

When teachers have little knowledge of or connection to immigrant communities surrounding their school, they can start through community participation, such as attending festivals and cultural events and getting to know different people. Teachers can eat at restaurants that serve authentic cultural dishes, support theaters and businesses in the immigrant communities, and work hard to develop positive relationships with families of children attending the school. Specifically reaching out to families from immigrant communities disconnected from teachers' own personal backgrounds can be the beginning of reciprocal relationships that benefit families, teachers, and children.

7. Welcome Families to the Classroom

Acknowledging families when they enter the classroom might seem obvious to experienced early childhood educators, but immigrant families told us this was one of the main ways they felt welcomed into the preschool classroom. They want to feel that their presence in the classroom and at the school is welcome and appropriate. Greeting families and spending time with them signals to families that they can freely ask the teacher questions, share concerns, or observe their children in the classroom.

Families explained that they understood much better what their children were learning when

they had the opportunity to observe and participate. Lilli in New York City said that she was worried about what the teachers had told her about learning through play, but that when she could see the learning taking place in the classroom, she understood how this type of learning worked.

Suggestions

When saying hello to families, smile and nod when they come in the room and approach them as soon as possible so they feel that they are in the right place and are welcome. Opening a classroom so that families can come to visit or volunteer during the school day makes it possible for more families to observe and become involved. This is important for immigrant families who, for linguistic,

Resources for Partnering with Refugee and Immigrant Communities

Refugees who have fled their countries due to persecution are a relatively small but extremely diverse group of immigrants. According to the United Nations High Commissioner for Refugees (UNHCR 2018), 25.4 million refugees were forced from their homes in 2017, the highest number ever recorded. In recent years, refugees admitted to the United States through the US Refugee Admissions Program (USRAP) came from about 80 countries and collectively spoke over 200 languages, with the majority from Syria, Iraq, Burma, Bhutan, Somalia, and the Democratic Republic of Congo (Capps et al. 2015; RPC 2018). Since USRAP resettles refugees throughout all 50 states, this "growing superdiversity" (Park, Zong, & Batalova 2018, 1) is reflected in large and small communities throughout the country, including early childhood education spaces.

Refugee families arrive with a great deal to contribute to their new home, and they tend to place a high value on their children's success in education. Research shows that children in immigrant families benefit from early childhood education; however, refugee children are

underrepresented in early childhood programs due to cultural and linguistic differences as well as practical barriers, such as insufficient information about US early care and education systems, cost of services, lack of transportation, and conflicts between family work schedules and center hours (Morland et al. 2016; Park & McHugh 2014).

In 2009, the National Association for the Education of Young Children (NAEYC) stated that "linguistic and cultural diversity is an asset, not a deficit, for young children," and presented key principles for serving diverse families (NAEYC 2009, 1). The principles include the importance of providing a welcoming environment, maintaining family and cultural connections, and helping children continue to develop their home languages while learning English. However, early childhood education programs may be unfamiliar with how to implement culturally and linguistically responsive practices, particularly given the current diversity of cultures and languages among families, as well as such practical considerations as limited funding and staff time.

cultural, or economic reasons, may be hesitant or unable to visit their children's school but are curious about what classrooms look like and how they function in the United States (Rodríguez-Brown 2009). Requiring families to schedule classroom visits may deter them from visiting if they suddenly have a day free, a longer break, or some unexpected free time. This doesn't mean that teachers need to feel that their classroom is constantly chaotic but that families know they are welcome to visit and volunteer in the classroom. In the beginning of the year, teachers can make it especially clear to immigrant families that they are welcome anytime and then demonstrate it when they arrive.

Recognizing and Valuing Immigrant Families and Immigrant Communities

For schools, teachers, and programs that wish to strengthen their relationships with immigrant families and their communities, we recommend finding ways to seek information and expertise from immigrant families before implementing programs, policies, or new initiatives. Some schools in our study created mentorship programs in which alumni immigrant families partner with new immigrant families to learn about early education. New families welcomed this opportunity to share their thoughts about early education with other immigrant families. Teachers who do not share linguistic or cultural ties with the children they teach can seek guidance, cultural insights, and expertise from immigrant teachers or immigrant community members (Adair 2011). Monolingual teachers can spend time in and support immigrant communities, giving them insight into families' lives outside

Below are resources, codeveloped by Head Start and refugee resettlement agencies, that can be used to improve cultural and linguistic responsiveness across *all* early childhood programs and community-based organizations, not just those serving refugee and immigrant children:

> **Cultural backgrounders.** These resources provide broad background information on refugee families from Bhutan, Burma, Iraq, and Somalia and offer suggestions on how staff can begin conversations and build relationships with families. Each backgrounder includes eight sections that cover migration background, culture and religion, family and community structures, childrearing and development, guidance and discipline, school and education, health, and community leadership. They also include practice tips and companion resources on ways to use the backgrounders in classrooms. While general knowledge is a good start in developing culturally responsive services, it is always best to learn, over time, each family's individual and unique background and

current context. https://eclkc.ohs.acf.hhs.gov/culture-language/article/cultural-backgrounders-various-refugee-cultural-groups-new-united-states

> ***Raising Young Children in a New Country: Supporting Early Learning and Healthy Development.*** Programs can use this resource to introduce families to early learning and child development knowledge in the United States. The illustrated handbook is divided into six themes: family well-being, health and safety, healthy brain development, early learning and school readiness, guidance and discipline, and family engagement in early care and education. Companion resources include the publication "Ways to Use the Handbook," which prepares providers to use the handbook through self-reflection and planning exercises, and "Tip Sheets" for exploring the different themes with families. https://eclkc.ohs.acf.hhs.gov/culture-language/article/raising-young-children-new-country-early-learning-healthy-development

(Adapted and updated from Morland & Levine 2016)

of the school. Teachers can support families' efforts to speak their home language at home by allowing children and family members to demonstrate their linguistic knowledge in the classroom (for an example of this, see Alvarez 2018).

It can be overwhelming to balance the increasing rigors of early childhood education settings with learning about, acknowledging, and including the cultures of communities different from your own. Showing authentic affection and patience for immigrant children, being respectful to the families and seeing them as experts, using their home language, and welcoming them to the classroom—as you welcome all families—aid in recognizing and valuing the voices of immigrant families.

Reflection Questions

1. Does your program serve immigrant families and communities? How have immigration patterns changed in recent years in your community?

2. What strategies do you use to learn more about immigrant families and communities and support them effectively?

3. How does the information shared in this article influence your programming?

4. Which of the seven suggestions from immigrant families do you feel your classroom or program can implement immediately? Which do you think will require more long-term planning?

5. Are there any agencies or organizations in your community that could help you strengthen your cultural responsiveness?

(Adapted from Morland & Levine 2016)

Conclusion

Perhaps this goal of listening to families is best exemplified by a teacher who works closely with the immigrant families in her classroom. She never assumes she fully understands a family but instead seeks relationships that help her be the best teacher possible for the children in the classroom.

I think it makes a difference when we try to get to know a family because, regardless of the culture, sometimes we don't understand what is happening. We try to build a relationship with the families because knowing and talking with them may be the lost link, the piece of the puzzle that was missing.

Listening carefully to families means taking their ideas seriously and seeing them as experts on their own children. When teachers work hard at developing relationships with immigrant families, they can more actively and positively serve the young children of immigrants in their classrooms.

References

Adair, J.K. 2011. "Confirming *Chanclas*: What Early Childhood Teacher Educators Can Learn From Immigrant Preschool Teachers." *Journal of Early Childhood Teacher Education* 32 (1): 55–71.

Alvarez, A. 2018. "Drawn and Written Funds of Knowledge: A Window into Emerging Bilingual Children's Experiences and Social Interpretations Through Their Written Narratives and Drawings." *Journal of Early Childhood Literacy* 18 (1): 97–128.

Arzubiaga, A.E., & J. Adair. 2010. "Misrepresentations of Language and Culture, Language and Culture as Proxies for Marginalization: Debunking the Arguments." Chap. 20 in *Handbook of Latinos and Education: Theory, Research, and Practice,* eds. E.G. Murillo Jr., S.A. Villenas, R.T. Galván, J.S. Muñoz, C. Martínez, & M. Machado-Casas, 301–308. New York: Routledge.

Aud, S., M. Fox, & A. KewalRamani. 2010. *Status and Trends in the Education of Racial and Ethnic Groups (NCES 2010-015).* Report. Washington, DC: US Department of Education, National Center for Education Statistics. www.nces.ed.gov/pubs2010/2010015.pdf.

Cahnmann-Taylor, M., & M. Souto-Manning. 2010. *Teachers Act Up! Performing Our Lives, Enacting Change.* New York: Teachers College Press.

Capps, R., K. Newland, S. Fratzke, S. Groves, M. Fix, M. McHugh, & G. Auclair. 2015. *The Integration Outcomes of U.S. Refugees: Successes and Challenges.* Report. Washington, DC: Migration Policy Institute. www.migrationpolicy.org/research/integration-outcomes-us-refugees-successes-and-challenges.

Derman-Sparks, L., & P.G. Ramsey. 2011. *What If All the Kids Are White? Anti-Bias Multicultural Education with Young Children and Families.* 2nd ed. New York: Teachers College Press.

Eeds, M., & G. Wells. 1989. "Grand Conversations: An Exploration of Meaning Construction in Literature Study Groups." *Research in the Teaching of English* 23 (1): 4–29.

Goodwin, A.L., & M. Genor. 2008. "Disrupting the Taken-for-Granted: Autobiographical Analysis in Preservice Teacher Education." Chap. 13 in *Diversities in Early Childhood Education: Rethinking and Doing,* eds. C. Genishi & A.L. Goodwin, 201–18. New York: Routledge.

Goodwin, A.L., R. Cheruvu, & C. Genishi. 2008. "Responding to Multiple Diversities in Early Childhood Education: How Far Have We Come?" Chap. 1 in *Diversities in Early Childhood Education: Rethinking and Doing,* eds. C. Genishi & A.L. Goodwin, 3–10. New York: Routledge.

Kersey, K.C., & M.L. Masterson. 2009. "Teachers Connecting With Families—In the Best Interest of Children." *Young Children* 64 (5): 34–38.

Ladson-Billings, G. 1995. "But That's Just Good Teaching!: The Case for Culturally Relevant Pedagogy." *Theory Into Practice* 34 (3): 159–165.

Lindfors, J.W. 1999. *Children's Inquiry: Using Language to Make Sense of the World.* New York: Teachers College Press.

Long, S., C. Anderson, M. Clark, & B. McCraw. 2008. "Going Beyond Our Own Worlds: A First Step in Envisioning Equitable Practice." Chap. 16 in *Diversities in Early Childhood Education: Rethinking and Doing,* eds. C. Genishi & A.L. Goodwin, 253–69. New York: Routledge.

Marinak, B.A., M.J. Strickland, & J.B. Keat. 2010. "A Mosaic of Words: Using Photo-Narration to Support All Learners." *Young Children* 65 (5): 32–36, 38.

Morland, L., N. Ives, C. McNeely, & C. Allen. 2016. *Providing a Head Start: Improving Access to Early Childhood Education for Refugees.* Report. Washington, DC: Migration Policy Institute. www.migrationpolicy.org/research/providing-head-start-improving-access-early-childhood-education-refugees.

Morland, L., & T. Levine. 2016. "Collaborating with Refugee Resettlement Organizations: Providing a Head Start to Young Refugees." *Young Children* 71 (4): 69–75.

NAEYC. 2009. "Where We Stand on Responding to Linguistic and Cultural Diversity." Position statement supplement. Washington, DC: NAEYC. www.naeyc.org/sites/default/files/globally-shared/downloads/PDFs/resources/position-statements/diversity.pdf.

Nagel, N.G., & J.G. Wells. 2009. "Honoring Family and Culture: Learning From New Zealand." *Young Children* 64 (5): 40–44.

New, R.S., & B.L. Mallory. 1994. "The Ethic of Inclusion." In *Diversity and Developmentally Appropriate Practices: Challenges for Early Childhood Education,* 2nd ed., eds. B.L. Mallory & R.S. New. New York: Teachers College Press.

Nieto, S. 2010. *The Light in Their Eyes: Creating Multicultural Learning Communities* (10th anniversary ed.). New York: Teachers College Press.

Park, M., & M. McHugh. 2014. *Immigrant Parents and Early Childhood Programs: Addressing Barriers of Literacy, Culture, and Systems Knowledge.* Report. Washington, DC: Migration Policy Institute. www .migrationpolicy.org/research/immigrant-parents-early-childhood-programs-barriers.

Park, M., J. Zong, & J. Batalova. 2018. *Growing Superdiversity Among Young U.S. Dual Language Learners and Its Implications.* Report. Washington, DC: Migration Policy Institute. www.migrationpolicy.org /research/growing-superdiversity-among-young-us-dual-language-learners-and-its-implications.

Rodríguez-Brown, F.V. 2009. *The Home–School Connection: Lessons Learned in a Culturally and Linguistically Diverse Community.* New York: Routledge.

RPC (Refugee Processing Center, US Department of State Bureau of Population, Refugees, and Migration). 2018. "Arrivals by Region." Last modified September 30. www.wrapsnet.org/admissions-and-arrivals.

Souto-Manning, M. 2010. "Challenging Ethnocentric Literacy Practices: (Re)Positioning Home Literacies in a Head Start Classroom." *Research in the Teaching of English* 45 (2): 150–78.

Souto-Manning, M. 2013a. *Multicultural Teaching in the Early Childhood Classroom: Approaches, Strategies, and Tools, Preschool–2nd Grade.* New York: Teachers College Press.

Souto-Manning, M. 2013b. "Teaching Young Children from Immigrant and Diverse Families." *Young Children* 68 (4): 72–80.

Souto-Manning, M., & R. Cheruvu. 2016. "Challenging and Appropriating Discourses of Power: Listening to and Learning from Successful Early Career Early Childhood Teachers of Color." *Equity and Excellence in Education* 49 (1): 9–26.

Souto-Manning, M., & J. Martell. 2016. *Reading, Writing, and Talk: Inclusive Teaching Strategies for Diverse Learners, K–2.* New York: Teachers College Press.

Tobin, J., A.E. Arzubiaga, & J.K. Adair. 2013. *Children Crossing Borders: Immigrant Parent and Teacher Perspectives on Preschool for Children of Immigrants.* New York: Russell Sage Foundation.

Tobin, J., Y. Hsueh, & M. Karasawa. 2009. *Preschool in Three Cultures Revisited: China, Japan, and the United States.* Chicago: University of Chicago Press.

Tobin, J.J., D.Y.H. Wu, & D.H. Davidson. 1989. *Preschool in Three Cultures: Japan, China, and the United States.* Binghampton, NY: Vail-Ballou.

UNHCR (United Nations High Commissioner for Refugees). 2018. *Global Trends: Forced Displacement in 2017.* Report. Geneva, Switzerland: UNHCR. www.unhcr.org/5b27be547.pdf.

Yosso, T.J. 2006. *Critical Race Counterstories Along the Chicana/Chicano Educational Pipeline.* New York: Routledge.

About the Authors

Jennifer Keys Adair, PhD, is an associate professor of early childhood education at The University of Texas at Austin. As a young scholar fellow with the Foundation of Child Development and a major grant recipient of the Spencer Foundation, she focuses on the connection between agency and discrimination in the early learning experiences of children of immigrants.

Alejandra Barraza, PhD, is the network principal of Carroll and Tynan Early Childhood Centers in the San Antonio Independent School District. Her dissertation work at The University of Texas at Austin compared the perspectives of superintendents, district-level administrators, and school/building administrators on early childhood practices. Alejandra formerly served as a teacher and an intern at the US Department of Education's Office of Early Learning.

Challenging Gender Stereotypes
A Teacher's Reflections on Counteracting Gender Bias

Nadia Jaboneta, with Deb Curtis

I was very excited about assembling a new contraption for the children to explore at the sensory table. I had a vision of what it would look like: funnels, chutes, many types of shovels, and lots of sand. As I began putting together different pipes and connectors, one of the children said, "Nadia, do you want me to ask my dad to come help you?" I responded, "That is so kind of you, but I am okay."

I continued to connect tubes, and then another child said, "I can ask my dad to come help you. He is a really good builder." I replied, "Thank you so much, but I can do this on my own."

Shortly after that, a third child came up to me and said, "Should I go get Randy to help you? He is really strong, and he likes building things."

I took a moment to think, and then I said, "Let's take a pause, everyone. I am hearing you say that I need a man to help me build this successfully. I want to let you all know that I am a strong and competent woman, and I believe I can do this by myself. Who are some powerful women that you know?" When there was no response, I said, "Looks like we have some work to do!"

Challenging Gender Stereotypes: A Teacher's Reflections on Counteracting Gender Bias

71

Nadia's Reflections

I care deeply about addressing bias, including gender bias, in our classroom and in the early childhood field. These interactions with the children made me aware that even in a progressive school such as mine, we may be unintentionally reinforcing biases and stereotypes. As I reflected on this situation, I wondered where the children's ideas were coming from.

I know that between the ages of 3 and 5, children begin to adopt gender-stereotyped thinking about themselves and others (Derman-Sparks & Edwards 2010). The children's reactions while I engineered a structure, an undertaking society categorizes as more "masculine," was a powerful reminder that children are influenced by everything around them: television, books, advertisements, peer behavior, adult behavior, and more.

NADIA PUTTING THE TUBES ON THE SENSORY TABLE. YOU ARE POWERFUL NADIA!

I want to become more conscious of my own gender biases and stereotypes and how I might be reinforcing the children's developing ideas. I plan to use spontaneous moments as opportunities to help children learn. I will help guide the children's thinking about gender and stereotypes when such situations come up. I look forward to exploring with them the diverse roles that women and men have in our lives and in our community. The children and I will learn together how people can do almost anything they set their hearts and minds on!

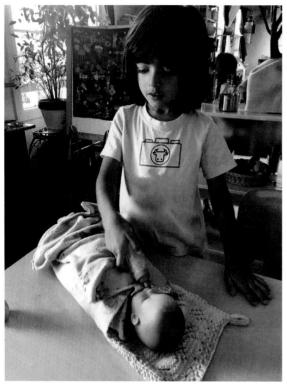 

Here are some actions I'll take to help counteract gender bias:

> Be mindful of the way I communicate with children. Am I speaking to girls and boys in different ways? Am I noticing behaviors in a gender-biased way or complimenting children in ways that reinforce stereotypes?

> Be aware of the gendered messages and images in our books, materials, and classroom, and take time to talk about any examples the children come across.

> Question stereotypes and generalizations about boys and girls that arise during the day.

> Continue to model behavior that challenges gender stereotypes and bring this behavior to the children's attention.

> Invite the children and their families to share stories and photos of themselves countering gender biases (aunt who is a construction worker, grandfather who is a nurse).

Reflection Questions

1. Conduct informal research in your classroom. Look at the books, materials, and displays. Do you notice any signs of stereotypical gender roles or gender biases? How do they counter gender stereotypes? Now observe the children to see whether their play and interactions reflect stereotypical gender roles or gender biases. Notice and reflect on how you help children see that girls and boys are capable of doing "anything they set their hearts and minds on."

2. What is your response when you see children in your group displaying stereotypical gender behavior and gender biases (girls not building in the block center, boys not playing with dolls)? What reasons do you have for your response?

3. As a teacher, what role do you play in countering biases and stereotypes with young children?

4. What do the children's responses to Nadia's work at the sensory table reflect about their skills and competencies in learning about the world around them?

5. Try some of Nadia's ideas. How do the children in your group think about gender differences? What impact do your actions have on their thinking and play?

Developed by Thinking Lens™

> Keep an eye out in our community for women and girls doing powerful things, and bring back photos and stories to share with the children (female politician giving a speech, sister winning a ribbon at the science fair).

> Learn more about how to help children develop age-appropriate skills that will help them think critically about gender issues and promote advocacy.

Reference

Derman-Sparks, L., & J.O. Edwards. 2010. *Anti-Bias Education for Young Children and Ourselves.* Washington, DC: NAEYC.

About the Authors

Nadia Jaboneta is a program coordinator and classroom teacher at Pacific Primary preschool in San Francisco, California. She has 20 years of experience teaching young children, training teachers, consulting, and facilitating workshops on various topics in the field of early childhood education.

Deb Curtis has spent the past 45 years working with children and teachers in early childhood programs and currently is a mentor toddler teacher at Epiphany Early Learning Preschool in Seattle, Washington.

Photographs: pp. 71, 72, 73 (both), courtesy of the authors

Reading Books, Writing Books

Reading and Writing Come Together in a Dual Language Classroom

Paola Pilonieta, Pamela L. Shue, and Brian T. Kissel

In Ms. Leon's dual language preschool classroom of 3-, 4-, and 5-year-olds, the children speak English and Spanish as they create books. Some children write about Transformers, while others write about their families. A few of the children's books are collections of words, scribbles, or pictures. Even the books that look like "just scribbles" convey a message the young authors share with their teachers and other readers. In this classroom, the children read books and make books in multiple ways and languages.

These child-created books, regardless of the language they are written in, are all about topics relevant to the authors and cover the broad spectrum of the children's home lives, school lives, and popular cultural interests that bridge the two (Kissel 2011). As Rowe (2018) and Kissel (2018) explain, young children's writing is meaningful and purposeful, even when their writing does not represent actual letters or words. Typically, preschoolers' writing consists of scribbles, linear lines, letter-like forms, and strings of letters. They do not yet have a concept of words, but they do have a concept of the world. When asked, they can discuss their marks and the meaning of words. Preschoolers are capable of meaningful writing beyond printing the alphabet on worksheets and writing their names (Lynch 2011). Teachers can empower preschoolers by providing opportunities to engage in authentic writing.

Opportunities for authentic writing are important because early experiences with print affect children's later literacy development (Rowe 2018). When children have a sense of print knowledge, they understand that print can be used in an array of social transactions and that print carries meaningful information (Purcell-Gates 1995). Additionally, writing and reading are interconnected processes (Drouin & Harmon 2009; Girard et al. 2013); thus, when children grow in one area, they can grow in the other as well.

Teaching Print Concepts Through Reading and Writing

Effective early childhood teachers capitalize on the connection between reading and writing by addressing literacy concepts from both a reading and a writing perspective. For example, when introducing children to print concepts, teachers typically use read-aloud sessions to demonstrate how to hold books and turn pages, where to start reading, the directionality of print, and the difference between a word and a letter. Teachers may then assess children's progress in understanding print concepts by observing how children handle books, inviting them to turn the pages during a read-aloud, or asking them to point out other features of print. In addition, when teachers observe children's knowledge of print concepts while they create books, an entirely new picture of each child's literacy development emerges.

In this article, we authors describe three dual language learners' (DLLs') knowledge of print concepts as they read and create books. These observations were collected as part of a larger research study about individual children's skills. We then present insights that teachers gain when they address reading and writing together.

Children in this classroom experience daily read-alouds and interact frequently with texts. They have daily opportunities to write based on topics and stories of their choice. As they write, the children talk in English, Spanish, or both. As part of our study, we authors and a literacy specialist meet individually with the children as they create books using marks and words to convey meaning. The literacy specialist, Johanna, is an important presence in the school—she models and observes instruction, serves as a coach, and engages in meaningful discussions with teachers about teaching. She also works with teachers to help them integrate literacy into the children's play.

Initially we ask children to discuss their books in both English and Spanish to ensure there is no language barrier. The conversation continues in the language in which the child is most comfortable. We take notes in both Spanish and English to record what the children are saying while they are composing.

In late winter, we give the children a book and ask them questions about basic print concepts (such as identifying a letter, a word, and the title of the book) in both English and Spanish. The results of these sessions for three children appear in "Concepts About Print Development in Reading and Writing" on page 78. This chart was created as part of the larger study.

Manuel: Bridges Between Emerging Reading and Writing

Manuel, who recently turned 5, speaks Spanish, is learning English, and enjoys attending a half-day preschool program. Manuel lives in a major urban city and comes from a family with a low income. While he has access to books at school, he has little access to books at home due to his family's low income and the limited number of texts available in his home language at the public library.

At first, we authors observe Manuel as he interacts with texts. Manuel has many interests (e.g., trucks, cars, Transformers) and is drawn to books on these topics. He shows a natural curiosity for learning and understands that books can be tools to help him learn about the world. When we watch him read a simple text, he attends solely to the picture on the page. He does not yet recognize the print on the page and, therefore, is not yet reading from left to right or following along the text with his finger. His writing style follows a similar pattern; most of his meaning is conveyed through drawings rather than letters and words, as is the case for most children his age.

During center time, Manuel grabs some markers and plain paper that has been stapled together as a blank book. Paola (one of this article's authors and the researcher) watches, walks over to him, and in Spanish asks him what he is going to do. He quickly responds that he is making a book about Transformers. As Manuel works, he turns the pages of the book from front to back. He draws on two pages, then goes back to write his name on the first page. He also draws and identifies himself as the author of the book. Manuel is deliberate with his drawings and marks, and when asked about these markings, he says that his book is about Transformers. He includes a drawing of a Transformer and surrounds that drawing with lines and dots, but he includes no written words in his story.

Manuel names the Transformers but there is no story structure or story line in his creation. Paola asks him, in Spanish, which is the front and back of the book, but he is not able to tell her. In addition, he does not differentiate between the print and the pictures on the page, nor does he write words other than his name. He knows what his book is about but does not give it a title. These examples indicate that Manuel's writing awareness is still

Concepts About Print Development in Reading and Writing

Concepts About Print	Manuel		Anita		Sofia	
	Reading	**Writing**	**Reading**	**Writing**	**Reading**	**Writing**
Title	Yes	Not Yet	Yes	Not Yet	Not Yet	Yes (verbally)
Word	Not Yet	Yes	Yes	Not Yet	Not Yet	Yes
Letter	Not Yet	Yes	Yes	Not Yet	Not Yet	Yes
Directionality of Print	Not Yet	Yes	Yes	Yes	Not Yet	Yes
Turns Pages	Yes	Yes	Yes	Not Yet	Not Yet	Yes
Holds Book Correctly	Yes	Yes	Yes	Not Yet	Yes	Yes

in the early stages. His limited oral storytelling ability in both languages is reflected in his writing ability. Both appear to be developing as he is learning two languages, which can be seen in "Concepts About Print Development in Reading and Writing." We also see Manuel's knowledge of print concepts when we ask him to identify concepts while he holds a book, and we assess his knowledge by observing his writing.

Though Manuel is still developing his understanding of print concepts, our observations of both his reading and writing skills offer a clearer picture of his development. Manuel understands that books convey a message and he sees himself as an author. Though he cannot yet identify letters in books, he can write his name. These observations highlight Manuel's emergent reading and writing skills. Offering him more meaningful opportunities in both reading and writing—for example, encouraging him to create his own Transformers stories—will continue to strengthen his literacy skills.

Anita: Reading as a Bridge Toward Writing

Anita is 5 ½ years old and, like Manuel, lives in the same urban area and is from a family with low income. She loves to talk and read in her home language, but she does not yet know many English words. At the time of our study, Anita is new to the United States, having arrived three months earlier. At home, her access to books is limited.

Anita demonstrates a strong awareness of print concepts while reading. She can identify the title of the book, letters, and words, and she understands print directionality (left to right). She holds books right-side up and turns the pages one at a time. When she reads her book to Paola, Anita uses inflection in her voice and reads with expression. Although Anita has good concepts about print knowledge with books, this does not transfer to her writing.

The researchers observe Anita's writing ability by encouraging her to make her own book. Anita eagerly takes the blank paper book and markers and sits down to create her story; however, she is unfamiliar with how to create the front and back of the book and she skips pages. When Paola asks her (in Spanish) "Can you point to the pictures?" and "Can you point to the words?," she cannot differentiate between them.

Anita draws pictures, but she does not include any scribbles, letter-like forms, letter strings, or anything else to indicate print on the cover or inside of the book. When Paola asks her in Spanish about her book, Anita says it is about herself, her house, and the flowers in her yard. Although Anita can articulate the meanings of her drawings, she is in the early development of print awareness when it comes to writing. She uses drawings to represent her ideas and relies on her oral language to explain and express her story.

Anita has good understanding of concepts about print when it comes to reading, but not when it comes to writing. She needs more writing experiences to further her awareness of how the print concepts she excels at when reading translate to writing. Anita's growing motivation to communicate her written message more clearly can propel her acquisition of writing skills, which will benefit both her reading and her writing.

Sofia: Writing as a Bridge Toward Reading

Sofia, a 5-year-old, speaks Spanish as her first language and is beginning to learn how to speak English. She lives in the same urban area as her peers and comes from a family of migrant workers. She will begin kindergarten in the fall, and her ability in reading and writing indicate her readiness for it.

When Johanna, the school's literacy specialist, assesses Sofia's concepts about print knowledge in English texts, she learns that Sofia shows little familiarity with books, print, and their purposes. Sofia holds books properly, but does not turn the pages and is unable to point to the title, a letter, or a word.

Before the assessment, Johanna observes Sofia in the writing center. While writing a book about her family in Spanish, Sofia turns the pages correctly, verbally tells Johanna the title of her story, and writes from left to right. She draws a picture of her family and then writes her father's name, indicating that she knows the difference between pictures and print, and that it is the print that carries much of the meaning. As a writer, she adds details to both the drawings and the print. On one page, Sofia exhibits a sophisticated sense of self-monitoring as she starts by writing *Joss*, realizes she has made a spelling mistake, crosses it out, and writes *José* (her father's name).

Sofia's literacy skills not only illustrate the importance of using both reading and writing when developing individual literacy profiles but also why observing children's use of these skills in their home language is critical. If we had relied only on the reading assessment, we would not have an accurate evaluation of what Sofia really knows about print. When Johanna assesses Sofia's knowledge of print concepts in both English *and* Spanish by looking at her writing, she realizes that Sofia knows much more about print than when Johanna looks only at how she reads books. The use of both languages demonstrates that when children are allowed to use their home language in the classroom, they can express more complex thinking and use more sophisticated skills than if they are permitted to only use their second language (Pilonieta & Medina 2009). Because she is given the opportunity to write in the language she is most comfortable with, Sofia is able to display her skills as a budding writer. Ms. Leon realizes the importance of supporting and scaffolding Sofia's literacy skills in Spanish. She knows that the writing knowledge and skills that dual language learners have in their home language frequently transfer to their English writing (August & Shanahan 2006; Feinauer, Hall-Kenyon, & Davison 2013; Spence 2010).

Implications for the Classroom

Manuel, Anita, and Sofia are representative of many preschoolers who enter classrooms reading, writing, and speaking one language and become dual language learners. But their emergence into literacy does not happen incidentally. Through supportive interactions with teachers, children learn to read and write in both their home language and in English in a number of ways.

Teaching Reading and Writing in Tandem

Young children naturally experience the synchronicity of reading and writing in their home and school lives. They read books by looking at and describing the images they see on the pages. Likewise, when they write, their messages are conveyed using printed pictures and scribbles, writing about the people and events of their lives using drawings. The two processes merge with one informing the other (Ray 2010). Most early childhood teachers recognize the important relationship between reading and writing and plan for them together.

Reading aloud to children can have a profound effect on their knowledge about writing and how their writing can inform audiences (Kissel & Baker 2008). When teachers read nonfiction texts aloud and discuss the content gleaned from the text, children might further explore the topics in their writing. We know that writing and reading develop together, and when children have opportunities to listen to a variety of texts read aloud (whether they are poems, stories, or magazine articles), they become familiar with different text structures. The more children read or listen to books read aloud, the better they are prepared to write.

In discussing the three children featured in this article, we build a case for finding ways to blend the teaching of reading and writing. When children read or listen to stories, they can also write stories and other forms of text in their own multimodal ways. Support children by making reading and writing part of their daily instruction, reading aloud and writing in front of the children, and honoring the reading and writing processes children use as they emerge into literacy. In the same way children make choices for reading, they should be empowered to do so when writing as well. For example, just as we encourage children to explore books that interest them, we should encourage children to write about topics that interest them as well. And when preschoolers are immersed in the engaging act of listening to and imagining elaborate stories, they can create their own stories that help them understand the role of characters, settings, and simple plots. Share your own writing with children, or conduct shared writing experiences with them.

Bridging Reading and Writing by Making Books

One of the ways young children understand the world around them is by reading books. They scan the pages, look at pictures, and formulate meaning using the pictures as clues. Making books allows young children to write, energizes them by writing for real audiences like peers and family members, and lets them grow as writers along their own individual developmental continuum (Ray & Cleaveland 2018). Making books is a perfect opportunity to connect reading with writing.

Create classroom spaces where bookmaking is routine. Often housed within the literacy center, a place for publishing offers tools and space for children to explore all the concepts of print by creating print themselves. Be sure your bookmaking center is stocked with a variety of materials for children to choose from, including different types of paper, writing instruments (e.g., pencils, markers, crayons, colored pencils, paintbrushes), and supplemental tools (e.g., stencils, staplers, hole punchers).

To see themselves as authors, children must *be* authors. Crafting books that serve authentic purposes and are read by audiences is an effective way to help children develop an author identity. With support from teachers, children can develop purposes for their writing (making a photograph-filled book for their classmates) as well as audiences for their finished products (classmates who missed a field trip can learn about the experience). As a result, the thinking–writing–publishing process becomes a natural experience for children. They might refer to an informational book about dinosaurs while writing their own dinosaur book and strategically place their book near the miniature fossil replicas in the science area. They might write simple memoirs about their lives and place their books alongside those written by Arthur Dorros, Sandra Cisneros, and Cynthia Rylant on the bookshelf.

Dual language learners, who have the benefit of knowing and communicating in two languages, can bring their own rich knowledge of words into this environment. It is important that teachers ensure that DLL writers are part of a supportive classroom community that recognizes their varied experiences and allows them to take risks. Such settings teach lessons that honor, support, and value DLLs' home languages as they simultaneously learn a second language (Laman 2013).

When children grow as authors, they grow as readers. As children learn how print works, learn about different types of text, and learn to read new words, they will want to explore and apply their new understandings to writing. Our role as teachers is to encourage this natural inclination.

Conclusion

While this article describes a bilingual setting where children are learning both English and Spanish, the practices shared here are applicable to *all* settings. Whether they are DLLs or monolingual, preschoolers develop literacy skills in similar ways (Laman 2013). Experiences that are effective for DLLs are also effective for children who speak only one language (Dennis & Votteler 2013). It is important to keep in mind that while their development is similar, DLLs are functioning in two languages and may take a little longer to demonstrate the same skill levels as monolingual children (Schulz 2009).

Ultimately, environments that provide many opportunities to interact with interesting and meaningful reading and writing activities enhance children's language and literacy development. For teachers of young dual language learners in particular, observing children reading and making books gives insights into children's literate lives and their lives outside the classroom. And this allows us to better understand and value the unique knowledge, skills, and experiences these children bring to the learning process.

Reflection Questions

1. How can you incorporate authentic writing opportunities into the classroom for the children you teach?

2. In the article, the children are assessed in both languages they are learning. Oftentimes, however, teachers do not speak the home languages of their students. Despite this barrier, how might you discover what the children already know about literacy when they enter your classroom?

3. How can you help children in your classroom develop reading and writing skills in concert with each other?

4. Why do you think it is important for young children to identify themselves as authors?

5. Think about your classroom environment and practices. What might you change to better support dual language learners' reading and writing skills?

References

August, D., & T. Shanahan, eds. 2006. *Developing Literacy in Second-Language Learners: Report of the National Literacy Panel on Language-Minority Children and Youth.* Mahwah, NJ: Erlbaum.

Dennis, L.R., & N.K. Votteler. 2013. "Preschool Teachers and Children's Emergent Writing: Supporting Diverse Learners." *Early Childhood Education Journal* 41 (6): 439–46.

Drouin, M., & J. Harmon. 2009. "Name Writing and Letter Knowledge in Preschoolers: Incongruities in Skills and the Usefulness of Name Writing as a Developmental Indicator." *Early Childhood Research Quarterly* 24 (3): 263–70.

Feinauer, E., K.M. Hall-Kenyon, & K.C. Davison. 2013. "Cross-Language Transfer of Early Literacy Skills: An Examination of Young Learners in a Two-Way Bilingual Immersion Elementary School." *Reading Psychology* 34 (5): 436–60.

Girard, L.-C., L. Girolametto, E. Weitzman, & J. Greenberg. 2013. "Educators' Literacy Practices in Two Emergent Literacy Contexts." *Journal of Research in Childhood Education* 27 (1): 46–60.

Kissel, B. 2018. "Listen, Ask, and Study: Reimagining How We Interpret Writing." *Language Arts* 95 (4): 242–47.

Kissel, B.T. 2011. "'That Ain't No Ninja Turtles': The Prevalence and Influence of Popular Culture in the Talk and Writing of Prekindergarten Children." *NHSA Dialog* 14 (1): 16–36.

Kissel, B., & M. Baker. 2008. "The Role of Informational Text in the Writing of Pre-kindergarten Children." *Balanced Reading Instruction* 15 (1): 75–89.

Laman, T.T. 2013. *From Ideas to Words: Writing Strategies for English Language Learners.* Portsmouth, NH: Heinemann.

Lynch, J. 2011. "An Observational Study of Print Literacy in Canadian Preschool Classrooms." *Early Childhood Education Journal* 38 (5): 329–38.

Pilonieta, P., & A.L. Medina. 2009. "Meeting the Needs of English Language Learners in the Middle and Secondary Classroom." Chap. 7 in *Literacy Instruction for Adolescents: Research-Based Practice,* eds. K.D. Wood & W.E. Blanton, 125–43. New York: Guilford.

Purcell-Gates, V. 1995. *Other People's Words: The Cycle of Low Literacy.* Cambridge, MA: Harvard University Press.

Ray, K.W. 2010. *In Pictures and In Words: Teaching the Qualities of Good Writing Through Illustration Study.* Portsmouth, NH: Heinemann.

Ray, K.W., & L.B. Cleaveland. 2018. *A Teacher's Guide to Getting Started with Beginning Writers.* Portsmouth, NH: Heinemann.

Rowe, D. 2018. "The Unrealized Promise of Emergent Writing: Reimagining the Way Forward for Early Writing Instruction." *Language Arts* 95 (4): 229–37.

Schulz, M.M. 2009. "Effective Writing Assessment and Instruction for Young English Language Learners." *Early Childhood Education Journal* 37 (1): 57–62.

Spence, L.K. 2010. "Generous Reading: Seeing Students Through Their Writing." *The Reading Teacher* 63 (8): 634–42.

About the Authors

Paola Pilonieta, PhD, is associate professor of reading and elementary education at the University of North Carolina at Charlotte. Her research includes early literacy instruction, literacy instruction for dual language learners, and teacher education and professional development.

Pamela L. Shue, EdD, is deputy superintendent of early education at the North Carolina Department of Public Instruction. She has served as a principal, special education teacher, and researcher.

Brian T. Kissel, PhD, is associate professor of reading and elementary education at the University of North Carolina at Charlotte. He researches early literacy in preschool and primary grades.

Becoming Upended

Teaching and Learning About Race and Racism with Young Children and Their Families

Kirsten Cole and Diandra Verwayne

At the beginning of the year in Ms. Verwayne's kindergarten class, the children are working on an All About Me project. They begin by drawing pictures of themselves based on observations of their reflections in a mirror. Next, the teacher provides them with sentence starters asking them to describe their hair color and texture, their skin color, and their eye color. In this racially and ethnically diverse class, the children learn a variety of vocabulary words they can use to describe these differences.

On the playground after school, some of the children's families chat about the project. One White mom, Ellie, tells the other families that the project made her feel a little uncomfortable. She explains, "Since this is the beginning of the year, shouldn't the kids be doing things that help them see what they have in common, rather than emphasizing their differences?"

Many families and teachers of young children share Ellie's concern that children should be shielded from learning explicitly about race and racial differences. Adults often worry that introducing these topics too early could be harmful (Husband 2010). Early childhood educators who wish to make space for learning about race and racism in their classrooms may feel unprepared to approach these complex issues (Vittrup 2016). Shaped by their own experiences with issues of race and racism, families and teachers may hold differing views regarding the appropriateness of teaching about this topic in the early childhood classroom.

Research demonstrates that children's awareness of racial differences and the impact of racism begins quite early (Tatum 2003; Winkler 2009). Multiple studies document the ways that young children take notice of racial differences and note that as early as preschool, children may begin excluding their peers of different races from play and other activities (Winkler 2009). Many argue that creating safe spaces for children to explore these topics is more important than ever, given the current political and cultural climate, where these issues are highly visible (Harvey 2017; Pitts 2016; Poon 2017). As such, families and teachers have an obligation to teach and learn with children about these critical and complex issues (Delpit 2012; Derman-Sparks, LeeKeenan, & Nimmo 2015; Ramsey 2015). This article documents how one kindergarten teacher, Diandra Verwayne (the second author), worked with the families in her classroom to grow *together* in their understandings of the role we all must play in talking with young children about race and racism. Additionally, this piece offers curricular and pedagogical resources for adults who are committed to engaging with young children in this crucial work.

Learning About Race and Unlearning Racism

In her seminal research and writing on this topic, Beverly Daniel Tatum (a former psychology professor and president of Spelman College) has written extensively about the ways in which the unjust structure of racial hierarchy in American society is normalized and transmitted to children from birth (Tatum 2003). In discussing how messages about race-based privilege and oppression are internalized, Tatum provides a powerful metaphor. She explains that in the same way residents who live in highly polluted areas cannot avoid becoming "smog breathers," Americans who are immersed in the structures and practices of white supremacy unwittingly become "racism breathers" (6). Many of us may not realize the degree to which these toxic beliefs shape our perceptions and experiences of the world. Unless we have opportunities to unlearn racism, these messages become absorbed and have consequences.

More recently scholars have documented the negative impact that being subjected to racism has on young children's academic success, as Lisa Delpit (2012) conveys in her aptly titled book chapter, "There Is No Achievement Gap at Birth." These consequences vary depending on our levels of privilege and oppression, which intersect across our diverse identities. Early childhood educators can support the unlearning of racism—and minimize later breathing in of racism— by intentionally teaching about race and related issues. Schools, in collaboration with families, have an important role to play in fostering young children's positive racial identities. Teachers who intentionally plan curricula that affirm children's racial identities have seen the benefits this produces in supporting children's growth and learning across many domains of development (Ladson-Billings 2009; Wright, Counsell, & Tate 2015).

There is often confusion about the difference between racially based bias and racism. Racism is a system of oppression that results from a combination of prejudice *and* power. This combination produces institutional structures and social practices that deny equity to people based on race. There is a common misconception that biases or prejudices that some people of color hold against White people constitutes "reverse racism." Anyone can hold a bias against people of another race, but only some races are subject to oppressive structures and practices as a result of that bias. To illustrate, consider a comparison to sexism. Some women are biased against men, but this is not "reverse sexism;" only men's biases against women have produced the conditions in which women are subjected to far more sexual harassment and sexual violence than men (Breiding et al. 2014). Similarly, racism has created structures and practices that deny equity and justice to people of color, including, for example, great disparities by race in family wealth. One of the most reliable ways to accumulate and pass on family wealth is through home ownership. Until recently, many Black Americans—including those with high incomes—were unable to buy houses because of redlining, a practice by which banks refused to offer mortgages in predominately Black neighborhoods. This is a key factor explaining why

Lessons Learned

When planning to implement a curriculum that addresses issues of race and racism, consider the following:

> Identify colleagues who are also committed to a racial justice curriculum and work together. Alternatively, seek out communities online to support your teaching practice. Remember, you're not alone!

> Anticipate the kinds of concerns or misconceptions that children and families might have, and prepare in advance some strategies for responding.

> Recall experiences that have expanded your own thinking about these issues, and consider sharing the story of how your perspective has grown and changed.

> Make yourself available, either in person or over the phone, to communicate with families about their perspectives on the curriculum. Email communication can often amplify disagreements, so try to keep communication face to face, if possible.

> Model a stance of respectful openness. Even if you disagree, strive to set a tone that maximizes the possibilities for considering different viewpoints.

> Recognize that we—children, families, and colleagues—are all on a journey of growth with respect to these issues. Draw upon the ways that you scaffold children's learning in other areas and apply these skills when supporting others' growth.

median wealth for White families in the US is about $134,000, while the median wealth for Black families is about $11,000 (Jones 2017). This disparity in family wealth accumulated over several generations and will likely take several more generations to address; meanwhile, it continues to have broad implications for access to opportunity, such as families' ability to pay their children's college tuition.

For all children to understand that the effects of racism are not the fault of people of color, we need to address these issues early in children's lives. We begin by fostering the positive development of every child's racial identity. This work must be paired with opportunities for young children to learn where and how injustice and inequality operate in our society. When children are armed with this knowledge and these skills, they can begin to disrupt these systems and work toward building a more equitable society for all of us.

One Teacher's Work

Ms. Verwayne teaches kindergarten at a racially and economically diverse public school. Born in Guyana, she moved to the United States at the age of 6 and recalls that when she entered school, she was made to feel like an outsider because of cultural differences. She reported, "When I was in elementary school, I felt like I had to hide my culture so that I could be accepted by the masses. I don't want that to happen within my classroom. I want my kids to be able to recognize who they are." Ms. Verwayne is committed to affirming children's racial and cultural identities throughout the year.

In her planned curriculum, Ms. Verwayne begins by offering learning experiences that allow children to observe and celebrate their unique identities. She also acknowledges the need for teachers to reflect on potential questions and concerns in order to prepare (as much as possible) for unplanned teachable moments. While she knows that some adults may resist addressing topics like identity, race, and racism with young children, she remains committed to the idea that these issues are an essential part of the early childhood curriculum. Musing about this tension, she shared the questions she asks herself as she designs curriculum:

> If I do talk about race, will it offend anyone? How do you talk about it in a way that doesn't offend people? . . . I think a lot of teachers will just choose not to address it because if you don't address it, you're not offending anybody. . . . I think this is the problem that we have in our country. . . . We never have an honest, open discussion about race *ever.*

Considering the current climate in America, where racism and racially motivated violence are visible to adults and children, Ms. Verwayne feels the stakes are too high to ignore this topic in her classroom.

Responding to Families' Anxiety

Because Ms. Verwayne is committed to openly and collaboratively addressing these topics, she believes it is important to discuss families' concerns. For this article, two parents whose children were enrolled in Ms. Verwayne's kindergarten classroom were interviewed by Kirsten Cole (the first author) about the curriculum. Fabiola is a Haitian American mother of two. Ellie is a White mother of two. Both mothers' first-born children were in Ms. Verwayne's class.

After moving to the United States at the beginning of kindergarten, Fabiola was frequently the target of racial epithets and other acts of racism. Fabiola described the painful consequences of having internalized these oppressive messages, in large part because as a child she did not have the opportunity to process these experiences with her family or teachers. As a parent, Fabiola has prioritized giving her children many opportunities to celebrate their racial identity and making space for their questions about race and racism. Nonetheless, Fabiola recognizes the potential for some families, particularly those who are White, to feel uncomfortable with such a curriculum. She explained,

> I think the teachers have to be prepared to deal with the parents and manage the anxiety of the parents. Because I think instructionally and educationally teachers know that it's important. . . . I strongly believe that the kids can tolerate it. It's the parents that are the hardest to convince.

Given the tendency of some adults to avoid these topics, Fabiola was pleased to discover that Ms. Verwayne made learning about race an integral part of the curriculum.

Ellie, in contrast, expressed some initial resistance to having her daughter participate in open discussions of racial differences. Ellie grew up in the Midwest in mostly racially homogenous environments. As is the experience for many White children, Ellie recalled that race was never discussed. Echoing the "colorblind" view that many White families espouse, Ellie recounted, "I don't think I thought about it much. I always thought, 'Everybody's wonderful. Everybody's the same.'" When her daughter began to attend public school, Ellie and some of the other White families discussed their concerns about Ms. Verwayne's curriculum. Ellie recalled,

> In kindergarten they did a worksheet for social studies about identity. The worksheet asked them to note their physical traits: eye color, skin color, hair color, hair texture, things like that. That was the first time anything like this had come up. I was thinking, "What is this? This is ridiculous. There's no reason that 5-year-olds should be doing this sort of exercise. This is futile. Why should my kid be having to say that she's White?"

In recalling how she felt at the time of this incident, Ellie articulated a stance many White people are raised to adopt: claiming to not see color is the most equitable way to approach teaching and learning about race.

Especially in recent years, many scholars have questioned the presumed benefits of the colorblind approach (Husband 2012; Pollock 2005). As society is not equitable and racial bias does exist, the colorblind approach denies children the validity of their experiences of the world. Because the impact of racial bias is visible, not allowing children to process this injustice is confusing, and it denies them the opportunity to see themselves as agents of change to resist injustice. Colorblindness fails to acknowledge the impact of racism on all people and, further, does not push White people to do the important work of reckoning with the legacy of white supremacy in our lives (Derman-Sparks & Ramsey with Edwards 2011; DiAngelo 2012).

Ms. Verwayne has a practice of encouraging families to meet with her during weekly family engagement time. At one such meeting, she asked if anyone had any questions about the curriculum. Ellie responded, "Actually, there was a worksheet that came home, and I don't think this is a useful thing. I think it's really hurtful, because it makes them identify things they haven't even realized about each other." Ms. Verwayne recalled being surprised by Ellie's reaction to the assignment, but she was grateful to have the opportunity to open a dialogue about their different views. She explained, "I needed to understand where that parent was coming from, and that parent needed to understand where I was coming from." For her part, Ellie had the opportunity to hear both Ms. Verwayne's intentions and also other families' perspectives on the curriculum. Ellie recalled,

> Fabiola responded, "Well, as a Black woman, we take a lot of pride in who we are and we want to talk about it a lot." As soon as she said that I realized, "Oh, of course. You're proud of your race. And I am not."

Ellie's reflection on this experience revealed another tension the colorblind view often masks. In naming the root of her discomfort, Ellie illuminated one of many challenges teachers face when doing this work in schools. The false premise of colorblindness is often deployed to obscure the discomfort White people have with confronting ongoing and historical racial oppression and injustice (Harvey 2017). As Fabiola noted in a later interview, "I think it's really detrimental to tell children they don't see what they're seeing and they're not feeling what they just felt—that they can't trust their eyes and they can't trust their gut."

While Ellie had entered the conversation seeking to maintain the colorblind view, she suddenly realized that not speaking about race with children does not protect them. Having had the opportunity to see the issue from another perspective, Ellie reported being transformed. Reflecting on this incident in a later interview, she recalled,

> It was just totally eye-opening. It *upended* me. Ever since then I just thought, there are so many parents of both Black and White kids and kids of every race that need to have those conversations about these differences, and that the differences are good. I realized that it has to be talked about.

This transformation—this "upending"—would not have been possible had Ms. Verwayne not opened this potentially challenging dialogue with families.

Particularly in early childhood, it is essential to build trusting and respectful relationships with families. Not all families will be receptive to a curriculum that addresses these issues, nor will all families be as open to being transformed in their thinking, as Ellie was. Ellie remarked, "What I really appreciate about Ms. Verwayne is her openness and respect for different viewpoints. Whenever I have had a concern, she has always been willing to talk and listen to my position with great interest and care." For early childhood teachers seeking to do the critical work of teaching about race and racism, it is important to be prepared to address families' myriad responses, including being ready and willing to create space for conversations many of us have been taught to avoid. While some families may never be open to a new way of thinking, teachers who model this openness will set the tone for approaching disagreements respectfully. As Fabiola noted, the hesitation that many White families have stems from adults' issues rather than any difficulty children may have in exploring the topic (DiAngelo 2012). She mused,

> It's not a scary thing. It may be uncomfortable, but it's a good thing to be having this conversation at this stage. And it was fine. We pass on these anxieties to our kids. The more anxious we are in talking about it, the more anxious they feel. They think that there's something wrong with what they're saying.

It may be surprising that children are ready for us to facilitate these learning opportunities. As family members and teachers, it is critical that we make *ourselves* ready for planned and unplanned opportunities to learn about race and racism.

Following Children's Leads

As with the curriculum that sparked the previous discussions, teaching and learning about race should begin with children's observations. Children notice differences and need to feel safe and supported in asking questions about what they notice. Fabiola explained that her daughter's learning about race "has been very child directed. . . . If she asks a question, more times than not it's just an observation of something. So I acknowledge the fact that she's absolutely right. She's noticing differences." Ms. Verwayne concurred; she likes to follow children's leads and design projects, activities, and read-alouds that emerge from their questions and concerns. She emphasized that children's innate sense of justice and fairness creates opportunities for them to wrestle with these questions. She explained, "Their questions mean that they're seeking an answer about this topic. And they have a lot of curiosity and wondering, and they need a way to figure out that answer." As with other inquiry-based learning experiences, a curriculum that emerges from the children's process of making sense of the world often yields the most engaging opportunities for learning.

While some of children's observations and questions about racial differences may be straightforward, at times children echo harmful biases they have heard elsewhere. Ms. Verwayne recalled an afternoon when her class returned from lunch in a state of distress. One of her students, a Black American girl, had told another child, "I don't like White people." At the time, the nightly news was full of reporting about police brutality against Black Americans, so Ms. Verwayne suspected that the child was repeating something she had overheard an adult say. Though math was on the schedule for the afternoon, Ms. Verwayne asked the children to join her in a circle on the rug. Drawing upon strategies she had learned in Responsive Classroom workshops, she reminded the children of their classroom norms that create space for each child's voice. She reminded the children to use accountable talk grounded in their experiences and to listen to each other with care. As they shared their feelings about what had happened at lunch, Ms. Verwayne prompted them to reflect on the sense of community and friendship they had cultivated together in class. They concluded that, while some people of any race may "not always be nice," we cannot draw conclusions about a whole race based on the actions of individuals.

Using Literature as an Entry Point to Discussions About Race

There are a number of ways early childhood educators can approach race in the classroom, referred to here as *race-related teaching practices* (RRTPs). Children's literature offers an engaging vehicle for generating these conversations about race, which is part of a larger effort to revise conceptualization of high-quality early childhood education to include teaching practices that intentionally address race.

Books that provide readers with opportunities to see different aspects of themselves, their communities, and the people they love can serve as material tools that affirm their sense of racial identity (Yenika-Agbaw & Napoli 2011). Such books can serve as springboards for teachable moments and meaningful conversations reflecting the teacher's color awareness and orientation toward thinking and acting from a social justice perspective. It is important to remember, however, that no book can fully represent a group or a complex issue. Rather, it is helpful to think in terms of text sets, or collections of connected books, that address different perspectives on topics.

Consider the following scenarios—one in which a teacher uses a color-aware approach and the other in which a teacher uses a social justice approach.

Tasha comes to kindergarten, excited to share news that her baby brother has been born. Other children want to share stories about what happened when their siblings joined their families. Ms. Franklin asks the children to describe what babies look like and then reads *Happy in Our Skin*, by Fran Manushkin, illustrated by Lauren Tobia (2015), a poetic celebration of different skin tones.

The expressive words prompt the children to describe their own skin. "My skin is cinnamon," one child offers. "Mine is more cocoa," says another. Ms. Franklin affirms their observations: "Each of us is unique. We are different in lots of ways, including our races." She then takes out paint and guides the children as they mix colors to match their own skin.

In this snapshot, Ms. Franklin, using a color-aware approach, reads to the children from high-quality literature that addresses concepts related to racial differences in a positive manner. Second, she encourages them to respond to the text. Finally, she uses the

Planning for Learning Through Children's Literature

For families and teachers wishing to open a dialogue about racial identity and racism, children's literature provides an excellent starting point. Well-written children's literature allows children to identify with and develop empathy for characters, particularly those that may be different from themselves. Stocking the classroom library with children's books that represent a diversity of experiences is essential. Providing books that allow children to see themselves in the pages offers the kind of high-interest materials that support children's early literacy (Klefstad & Martinez 2013). Especially when children are beginning to do the challenging work of learning to read, it is important for them to be able to select books that allow them to feel a connection to the content. If children do not see their lives and interests reflected in the books in your library, they may feel that reading is not for them.

To foster an appreciation of difference and empathy, it is especially important to have a classroom library that represents a range of characters and experiences. Great children's books allow us to get inside the protagonists' experiences. Fortunately, excellent

Stocking Your Library with Equitable and Inclusive Children's Books

> Lee & Low Books: www.leeandlow.com

> Raising Race Conscious Children: www.raceconscious.org/childrens-books

> Social Justice Books: A Teaching for Change Project: www.socialjusticebooks.org/booklists

> We Need Diverse Books: www.diversebooks.org

opportunity to extend children's consideration of their racial identity by giving them the time, materials, and pedagogical support to extend their learning through an appropriate activity.

Let's look at another example of effective use of RRTPs and children's literature. Before story time, a first grade teacher has planned ways to help the children think about different aspects of the text, including issues related to race.

> Mr. Harkins gathers the children for a read-aloud of *Mr. George Baker*, by Amy Hest, illustrated by Jon J. Muth (2007), the story of a friendship across both age and race. In the text, young Harry is mesmerized by Mr. George Baker. At age 100, George has accomplished many things—he is a talented musician with a loving wife and a warm home. Yet he has never learned to read—a problem that he indicates "must be corrected." Harry and George are bound together in their pursuit of learning—Harry in the first grade and George in adult education.

> Afterward, individual children comment on different parts of the story. One child mentions his relationship with an older neighbor to whom he and his mother take treats. Another says, "George could really play!" He then stands and taps out his own rhythm, just as Mr. Baker does in the book. "It's too bad George never learned to read, but he's going to now—even though he's old," says another. Mr. Harkins smiles and says that they really noticed a lot. Then, he adds, "It's great that Mr. Baker is learning to read. Hmm . . . I wonder why he waited. Does anyone have thoughts on why he didn't learn to read before?"

Through his question, the teacher has opened up a social justice teaching moment. The children can consider possible reasons why Mr. Baker did not learn to read. Could it have been because he didn't finish school? Was he doing other things, like working or helping at home? Could it be that Mr. Baker was not welcomed at school? Did race play a part in this? By introducing important issues that might not be readily apparent, teachers provide children with opportunities to become critical readers who can move beyond the text of a book to read between the lines. They can use a social justice lens to view and discuss sensitive historical and current events.

(From Wanless & Crawford 2016)

resources exist to guide teachers and families in creating such libraries (see "Stocking Your Library with Equitable and Inclusive Children's Books" on page 93). The classroom library can offer a child-friendly opening to learn about important histories and to celebrate the accomplishments of seminal figures in the fight for racial equality. However, be sure to provide a balance and to also include books that represent diverse characters engaged in ordinary, everyday experiences.

Once you develop a classroom library that addresses issues of race and racism from many perspectives, prepare yourself to respond to children's questions as they arise. Ms. Verwayne recalled that when reading about the life of Dr. Martin Luther King, Jr., her children wanted to know more. When the book addressed the topic of segregation, they asked, "But why would people do that?!?" Ms. Verwayne was glad that she had anticipated these questions and was able to provide context by talking about Jim Crow and how it institutionalized racial bias and made it the law of the land.

Developing Strategies for Responding to Teachable Moments

In addition to planning a curriculum that addresses issues of race and racism, Ms. Verwayne described how she often needed to think on her feet in responding to children's natural curiosity about race and difference. Many teachers may have a desire to address these topics but feel unprepared to respond when the issues arise in their classrooms. Teachers need resources and support to develop the tools to do this work skillfully and thoughtfully. Ms. Verwayne argued that this includes trusting teachers to think on their feet and to ground their responses in the deep knowledge they have of their classroom communities. She noted,

> Some people definitely do not want to discuss issues of race and difference at all. They think it's best to sweep it under the rug and just act like it doesn't exist. That's the safest space to be in. But is it the *right* space to be in, knowing the times that we're in? I think we need to give teachers the leeway to be unconventional and try different ways to address this.

In an era when many educational reforms have argued for standardization and "teacher proofing" the curriculum, the work of responding to complex issues requires that we give teachers the training and time to reflect on and discuss them, and also trust teachers to write their own script when teachable moments arise.

As described earlier, Ms. Verwayne uses protocols and practices offered by the Responsive Classroom to facilitate a complex conversation about racial bias. By developing these routines, Ms. Verwayne asks the children to join her in taking ownership of creating the kind of classroom in which they all feel included. These pedagogical strategies are supported by the content of her social studies curriculum, which explores the meaning of community.

Preparing for and Responding to Teachable Moments

> Center for Racial Justice in Education: www.centerracialjustice.org

> National Association for the Education of Young Children's Anti-Bias Resources: NAEYC.org/topics/anti-bias-education

> Raising Race Conscious Children: www.raceconscious.org

> Responsive Classroom: www.responsiveclassroom.org

> *Rethinking Early Childhood Education,* by Ann Pelo (2008)

> Teaching Tolerance: www.tolerance.org

> *What If All the Kids Are White? Anti-Bias Multicultural Education with Young Children and Families,* Second Edition, by Louise Derman-Sparks and Patricia G. Ramsey, with Julie Olsen Edwards (2011)

A number of organizations have created forums for the exchange of social justice curriculum ideas (see "Preparing for and Responding to Teachable Moments" on page 94). Responding to teachable moments is never one size fits all; but resources that provide candid and thoughtful sharing of teacher knowledge can provide teachers with models of practices and strategies. Even pedagogical models that do not explicitly address race and racism, such as the practices offered by the Responsive Classroom, can be adapted to create a framework for talking about race in the classroom. Whatever the approach, we must acknowledge the need to offer these kinds of curricular and pedagogical strategies to teachers throughout their professional development experiences.

Conclusion

This article, along with the suggested resources, provides a starting point for teachers and families seeking to do the important work of supporting young children's learning and understanding about race and racism. As Ms. Verwayne's experiences illustrate, this work is both challenging and essential. Concluding her reflections on her own experiences with Ms. Verwayne's kindergarten, Ellie emphasized, "In a school where you don't have the kind of diversity we have, it might be even more important." As we prepare young children to be members of the human family, we must offer them opportunities to celebrate all aspects of their identities and to resist bias and oppression. In the field of early childhood education, we spend much of our time and energy nurturing children's capacity for kindness and respect. Helping children see the role they have to play in fostering equality and inclusion through racial justice is a critical piece of this project.

References

Breiding, M.J., S.G. Smith, K.C. Basile, M.L. Walters, J. Chen, & M.T. Merrick. 2014. "Prevalence and Characteristics of Sexual Violence, Stalking, and Intimate Partner Violence Victimization—National Intimate Partner and Sexual Violence Survey, United States, 2011." *Morbidity and Mortality Weekly Report: Surveillance Summaries* 63 (8): 1–18. www.cdc.gov /mmwr/preview/mmwrhtml/ss6308a1.htm.

Delpit, L. 2012. *"Multiplication Is for White People": Raising Expectations for Other People's Children.* New York: The New Press.

Derman-Sparks, L., D. LeeKeenan, & J. Nimmo. 2015. *Leading Anti-Bias Early Childhood Programs: A Guide for Change.* New York: Teachers College Press; Washington, DC: NAEYC.

Derman-Sparks, L., & P.G. Ramsey. With J.O. Edwards. 2011. *What If All the Kids Are White? Anti-Bias Multicultural Education with Young Children and Families.* 2nd ed. New York: Teachers College Press.

DiAngelo, R. 2012. "What Makes Racism So Hard for Whites to See?" Chap. 10 in *What Does It Mean to Be White? Developing White Racial Literacy,* 167–89. New York: Peter Lang.

Reflection Questions

1. Think about a time that you were "upended" in your perspective on issues of race. What aspects of this experience opened you to a different perspective? How did this experience change your approach to teaching?

2. What kinds of experiences could you facilitate for others (e.g., colleagues and families) that might expand their perspective on issues of race?

3. Why is it important for teachers working with children of color to address issues of race and racism in our work? Why is it important for teachers working in predominately White schools to address these issues? Are there different considerations in how we address these issues, depending on the demographics of the children we are working with?

4. Imagine that the family member of a child in your class comes to you and shares that they are uncomfortable with you teaching about issues of race and racism. What could you say or do that might open him up to understanding the value of this work?

5. Approximately 80 percent of the teaching workforce is White. White teachers' lives do not always provide them with perspective on people of color's experiences of race and racism. What can White teachers do to educate themselves about race and racism?

Harvey, J. 2017. "Are We Raising Racists?" Opinion, *New York Times,* March 14. www.nytimes.com/2017/03/14/opinion/are-we-raising-racists.html.

Husband, T. 2010. "He's Too Young to Learn About That Stuff: Anti-Racist Pedagogy and Early Childhood Social Studies." *Social Studies Research and Practice* 5 (2): 61–75.

Husband, T. 2012. "'I Don't See Color': Challenging Assumptions About Discussing Race with Young Children." *Early Childhood Education Journal* 39 (6): 365–71.

Jones, J. 2017. "The Racial Wealth Gap: How African-Americans Have Been Shortchanged Out of the Materials to Build Wealth." *Working Economics Blog,* Economic Policy Institute, February 13. www.epi.org/blog/the-racial-wealth-gap-how-african-americans-have-been-shortchanged-out-of-the-materials-to-build-wealth.

Klefstad, J.M., & K.C. Martinez. 2013. "Promoting Young Children's Cultural Awareness and Appreciation Through Multicultural Books." *Young Children* 68 (5): 74–81.

Ladson-Billings, G. 2009. *The Dreamkeepers: Successful Teachers of African American Children.* 2nd ed. San Francisco: Jossey-Bass.

Pitts, J. 2016. "Don't Say Nothing." *Teaching Tolerance* 54 (Fall): 46–49. www.tolerance.org/magazine/tt54-fall-2016/feature/dont-say-nothing.

Pollock, M. 2005. *Colormute: Race Talk Dilemmas in an American School.* Princeton, NJ: Princeton University Press.

Poon, O. 2017. "Our Schools Need to Teach a Fourth 'R': Racial Literacy." *Rewire,* March 1. www.rewire.news/article/2017/03/01/schools-need-teach-fourth-r-racial-literacy.

Ramsey, P.G. 2015. *Teaching and Learning in a Diverse World: Multicultural Education for Young Children.* 4th ed. New York: Teachers College Press.

Tatum, B.D. 2003. *Why Are All the Black Kids Sitting Together in the Cafeteria? And Other Conversations About Race.* Rev. ed. New York: Basic Books.

Vittrup, B. 2016. "Early Childhood Teachers' Approaches to Multicultural Education and Perceived Barriers to Disseminating Anti-Bias Messages." *Multicultural Education* 23 (3-4): 37–41.

Wanless, S.B., & P.A. Crawford. 2016. "Reading Your Way to a Culturally Responsive Classroom." *Young Children* 71 (2): 8–15.

Winkler, E.N. 2009. "Children Are Not Colorblind: How Young Children Learn Race." *PACE: Practical Approaches for Continuing Education* 3 (3): 1–8.

Wright, B.L., S.L. Counsell, & S.L. Tate. 2015. "'We're Many Members, but One Body': Fostering a Healthy Self-Identity and Agency in African American Boys." *Young Children* 70 (3): 24–31.

Yenika-Agbaw, V., & M. Napoli, eds. 2011. *African and African American Children's and Adolescent Literature in the Classroom: A Critical Guide.* 2nd ed. New York: Lang.

About the Authors

Kirsten Cole, PhD, is a teacher, researcher, and parent from Brooklyn, New York, and an associate professor of early childhood education at the Borough of Manhattan Community College, CUNY. Additionally, she chairs the Equity, Diversity, and Inclusion Committees for both of her children's public schools.

Diandra Verwayne, MS, is a 16-year veteran of New York City public schools. She teaches in Brooklyn and recently served on her school's Diversity Committee as a teacher representative.

Supporting Gay and Lesbian Families in the Early Childhood Classroom

Anna Paula Peixoto da Silva

When those who have the power to name and to socially construct reality choose not to see you or hear you . . . when someone with the authority of a teacher, say, describes the world and you are not in it, there is a moment of psychic disequilibrium, as if you looked in the mirror and saw nothing. It takes some strength of soul—and not just individual strength, but collective understanding—to resist this void, this non-being, into which you are thrust, and to stand up, demanding to be seen and heard.

—Adrienne Rich, *Blood, Bread, and Poetry: Selected Prose 1979–1985*

E arly childhood educators today work with an increasingly diverse population of children and families. This diversity can include children from nontraditional families, such as families headed by a single adult, families of divorced parents, families headed by a relative other than a parent, and families headed by gay or lesbian parents. Yet many early childhood educators have minimal access to training about ways to support nontraditional families—and specifically same-sex partnered families (Averett, Hegde, & Smith 2017; Jennings & Macgillivray 2011; Jennings & Sherwin 2008). This article provides practical strategies for supporting children and parents in gay and lesbian households.

Children's success within their communities is largely determined by socialization that begins early on. Families transfer their values and beliefs to children through modeling and language, which shapes children's views of themselves and of the world around them. While such enculturation serves to support children's psychosocial wellbeing, in some cases it isolates individuals and groups whose cultures differ from the perceived societal norm, placing young children at risk for long-term emotional and behavioral challenges (Oakley, Farr, & Scherer 2017; Yoon et al. 2013).

Families, which constitute the most basic component of young children's self-identities, are a central part of the early childhood curriculum (HRC Foundation 2018). Therefore, negative views of same-sex partnered families in early childhood settings can be damaging to young children and parents who may feel stigmatized or uncomfortable about participating in practices not supportive of their family identity.

The inclusion of nontraditional families in the early childhood curriculum often depends on individual teachers' understanding of its importance, prior training and mentoring, and comfort level in discussing issues such as homosexuality. Children of gay and lesbian parents who begin school life feeling pride in their family may be silenced by negative direct and indirect messages they receive, lowering some children's self-esteem (Hedge et al. 2014). Given that positive relationships between families and schools support children's social and academic development (Fedewa & Clark 2009; Goldberg & Smith 2017) and their later success in life, how can early childhood professionals support these children and their families?

Strategies for Providing Support

While it is difficult to precisely determine the number of children being raised by same-sex couples in the United States, given the reluctance by some families to divulge that information (Averett, Hegde, & Smith 2017) and issues with reporting (Tasker & Patterson 2007), it is estimated to be approximately 200,000 children, and that number continues to increase (Oakley, Farr, & Scherer 2017). For early childhood teachers to welcome and affirm such families, they need strategies that enable them to create safe spaces. The strategies presented in this article revolve around three main areas: communication, heightening bias awareness, and creating an inclusive environment.

Communication

Kelly, who teaches 4-year-olds, sends home "All About Me" books for families to work on together. The book contains sentences with blanks to be filled in with information about the children's homes, their favorite toys, favorite foods, and of course their families. Each page also has space for children to draw pictures.

When Jorge's family does not return their completed book, Kelly contacts Mario, the only parent listed on Jorge's school enrollment form. Mario tells Kelly that his family feels uncomfortable participating in the activity, but does not explain his reasons. Kelly later finds out that Jorge has two fathers. A strong advocate of family–school relationships, Kelly reaches out to Mario to resolve any concerns he has with the assignment. They schedule a meeting for the following week.

Opening a Dialogue with Families

Family engagement is critical to children's success. Communication that fails to recognize gay and lesbian families can lead them to feel unwelcome and unappreciated (Fisher & Kennedy 2012). For example, issues may arise if teachers rely on gender stereotypes to manage relationships, such as by requesting to speak to the female caregiver regarding children's emotional needs and the male caregiver regarding discipline. One effective method to address communication challenges and create inclusive, safe spaces for families is *skilled dialogue* (Barrera & Kramer 2009; Barrera, Kramer, & Macpherson 2012), an approach that supports collaborative communication, understanding, and connecting diverse perspectives. To engage in skilled dialogue, teachers connect with families by focusing on building relationships to achieve a desired outcome. Kelly, for example, prioritized the connection she wished to make with Jorge's family rather than focusing on the completion of Jorge's book. She

went into the meeting without a set agenda, open and ready to listen to and understand Jorge's family's perspective.

Early in their conversation, it became clear that Kelly and Mario had differing views regarding the book assignment. Kelly came to understand that she may have unintentionally excluded Jorge and his family by including references in the assignment to parents as a *mother* and a *father*. To resolve the problem, Kelly

1. Reflected on the beliefs, perceptions, and thoughts that shaped their individual perspectives

2. Remained open to collaborating with Mario

3. Acknowledged differences between her assumptions about family and Jorge's family

4. Remained open to and respectful of their different perspectives

5. Worked to create a third, inclusive solution that addressed the classroom's as well as Jorge's family's needs (Barrera & Kramer 2009)

The skilled dialogue approach allowed Kelly to collaborate with Mario in a respectful, reciprocal, and responsive manner. To establish respect, Kelly welcomed Mario and thanked him for taking time to meet with her. During the meeting, Kelly used statements such as "Can you tell me more?" and "I see" to indicate her openness to Mario's opinions. Kelly's respectful tone acknowledged the importance of Mario's perspective and experiences and created an environment where he felt safe to share his reasons for not discussing his family structure with the school earlier. It also allowed him to share stories about his role as a gay father. Learning about and acknowledging differences in Jorge's family structure and her own assumptions about family structure, without being judgmental, supported Jorge's family's identity and consequently affirmed Jorge's identity.

Kelly demonstrated that she valued Mario's contributions by listening attentively to his views and opinions. To establish reciprocity, she showed appreciation, interest, and curiosity about Mario's perspective on the family book. When Mario noted his disappointment with the book's focus on heterosexual families, Kelly asked him to explain what he meant rather than telling him what she intended the book to be about. Kelly used phrases such as "I really want to understand what this book means to your family" and "I never thought of the book in that way."

To respect the connection they made and to demonstrate responsiveness, Kelly remained open to finding common ground between Mario's

Books for Preschoolers About Gay and Lesbian Families

› *And Tango Makes Three,* by Justin Richardson and Peter Parnell, illustrated by Henry Cole (2005)

› *The Baby Kangaroo Treasure Hunt: A Gay Parenting Story,* by Carmen Martinez Jover, illustrated by Rosemary Martinez (2009)

› *Daddy, Papa, and Me,* by Lesléa Newman, illustrated by Carol Thompson (2009)

› *In Our Mothers' House,* by Patricia Polacco (2009)

› *Mommy, Mama, and Me,* by Lesléa Newman, illustrated by Carol Thompson (2009)

› *Monday Is One Day,* by Arthur A. Levine, illustrated by Julian Hector (2011)

› *Stella Brings the Family,* by Miriam B. Schiffer, illustrated by Holly Clifton-Brown (2015)

› *A Tale of Two Daddies,* by Vanita Oelschlager, illustrated by Kristin Blackwood and Mike Blanc (2010)

› *A Tale of Two Mommies,* by Vanita Oelschlager, illustrated by Mike Blanc (2011)

perspectives and her own. Her responsiveness to Mario's comments allowed them to move into what Barrera and Kramer (2009) refer to as a *third space*—a phase when the two can focus on their commonalities and when each person's perspectives and viewpoints are equally important.

Finding Solutions Together

Through skilled dialogue, Kelly and Mario coconstructed a solution that allowed Jorge to take part in the activity in a way that was respectful of his family. Their solution involved not only recreating the book, changing all references from *mother* and *father* to *parents* and/or *family members*, but also creating a more welcoming learning environment for everyone. Kelly did so by hanging pictures and posters in the classroom showing nontraditional families and reading stories featuring gay and lesbian families to the children (see "Books for Preschoolers About Gay and Lesbian Families" on page 100). They worked together to find a solution, and Kelly established a respectful rapport with Jorge's father that would shape their future interactions and would support Jorge's developing sense of identity.

Kelly's meeting with Mario highlighted the need to create activities that were inclusive of all families, not just those whose structures she was most familiar with. Reflecting on the meeting, Kelly realized she needed to spend more time exploring her own biases and the impact they might have on the children and families she worked with. She needed to examine her own background and reflect on past interactions with nontraditional families to understand and work through any biases she might have (Derman-Sparks & Edwards 2010).

Heightening Awareness of Bias

Kelly used the following questions to help guide her thinking:

> Based on my experiences, are there any implicit biases that may affect my interactions with children and their families?

> What does my use of language and choice of materials in the classroom indicate about the value and importance of diverse families—specifically, gay and lesbian families? (Duke & McCarthy 2009)

> Are there differences among people and families that make me uncomfortable? If so, what are they?

> How do I respond to differences among people and families?

> How do I respond to children's comments and questions about gender roles and identities?

Helpful Websites

> **AMAZE:** This nonprofit organization focuses on creating safe and respectful communities for all children. www.amazeworks.org

> **Children of Gays and Lesbians Everywhere (COLAGE):** This organization provides LGBTQIA+ families with a network of peers focused on establishing a sense of community and validating the family structure and shared experiences of LGBTQIA+ families. www.colage.org

> **Gay, Lesbian, and Straight Education Network (GLSEN):** This organization works to ensure that all students are valued and treated with respect and that school environments are focused on affirming identities and fostering personal growth and development. www.glsen.org

> **Teaching Tolerance:** This Southern Poverty Law Center project supports equitable school experiences for all children by providing free educational materials to teachers in the United States and Canada. www.tolerance.org

> **Welcoming Schools:** This site addresses ways to promote family diversity while reducing gender stereotyping, bullying, and name-calling. It offers administrators, educators, and families a variety of resources to create learning environments where all learners are welcomed and respected. www.welcomingschools.org

By answering these questions, Kelly realized that some of her past actions and language may have unintentionally conveyed an unwillingness to include all families. While she had always considered herself to be supportive of diverse children and families, that diversity had been limited to ethnicity and race. She realized that acknowledging her biases was the first step toward working through them.

Creating an Inclusive Environment

One important lesson Kelly learned from Mario was that families often choose to keep information about their family structure private. Specifically, she realized it was critical for her not to expect parents to self-identify as gay or lesbian before establishing a safe, inclusive environment for their children.

To provide a welcoming, accepting space that empowered children of same-sex partnered families, Kelly designed a classroom that was representative of children's identities and communicated the importance of all families. She worked to create an environment that was physically and emotionally safe for the children. That year, Kelly relied on Mario's assistance and information she researched online to select classroom resources and materials that positively represented gay and lesbian individuals and affirmed the children's experiences (see "Helpful Websites").

Kelly placed age-appropriate books depicting same-sex partnered families in the reading center. She also added multiple male and female persona dolls of various ages and ethnicities to different areas of the classroom to allow children to represent in their play different family experiences. Although Kelly had concerns about other families' reactions to the posters of same-sex partnered families placed around the classroom, she noticed that the images were interpreted differently by children and families. While children of same-sex partnered families saw two mothers or two fathers in the posters, other children saw a father and an uncle or friend and a mother and sister. If a family were uncomfortable with the posters, Kelly would respond by respecting their views while engaging them in skilled dialogue.

Other steps Kelly used to maintain an inclusive environment were

> Using inclusive language in all written and oral communication (e.g., addressing communication to children's families rather than to children's parents)

> Using terms such as *partner* instead of *husband* or *wife* when communicating with families

> Modeling respect for gay and lesbian families in all interactions and communication by listening attentively and addressing their needs

> Addressing children's comments and questions about different family structures with age-appropriate answers that focus on the love that brings families together

> Celebrating Family Day instead of Mother's Day or Father's Day

> Adapting finger plays and songs to include gay and lesbian families (e.g., changing the lyrics from Thomas Moore's "Family Jog" song from "Look at my father jog" to "Look at my fathers jog")

> Providing classroom materials (e.g., books, posters) to reflect families' unique contexts

The new environment and supportive behaviors Kelly modeled sent clear messages to Jorge's family about their importance . . . as well as the importance of everyone else's families.

Conclusion

Given the growing number of gay and lesbian households, it is important that we teachers examine our early childhood classroom practices to ensure that we create environments that welcome all types of families. There is a wealth of opportunities for collaborating and building relationships between teachers, schools, and families. This empowers children and strengthens our ability to respond to the families' diverse needs.

Reflection Questions

1. In your experience, what strategies have proven most effective in working with gay and lesbian families?

2. This article addresses the importance of communication, bias awareness, and construction of inclusive environments. In what other areas can you extend your work of supporting gay and lesbian families?

3. How do your program's policies demonstrate sensitivity to working with children of gay and lesbian families?

4. How do your current practices support a welcoming environment for all types of families?

5. What immediate steps can you take to ensure all families feel welcome and supported in your classroom?

References

Averett, P., A. Hegde, & J. Smith. 2017. "Lesbian and Gay Parents in Early Childhood Settings: A Systematic Review of the Research Literature." *Journal of Early Childhood Research* 15 (1): 34–46.

Barrera, I., & L. Kramer. 2009. *Using Skilled Dialogue to Transform Challenging Interactions: Honoring Identity, Voice, and Connection*. 2nd ed. Baltimore: Brookes.

Barrera, I., L. Kramer, & D. Macpherson. 2012. *Skilled Dialogue: Strategies for Responding to Cultural Diversity in Early Childhood*. 2nd ed. Baltimore: Brookes.

Derman-Sparks, L., & J.O. Edwards. 2010. *Anti-Bias Education for Young Children and Ourselves*. Washington, DC: NAEYC.

Duke, T.S., & K.W. McCarthy. 2009. "Homophobia, Sexism, and Early Childhood Education: A Review of the Literature." *Journal of Early Childhood Teacher Education* 30 (4): 385–403.

Fedewa, A.L., & T.P. Clark. 2009. "Parent Practices and Home–School Partnerships: A Differential Effect for Children With Same-Sex Coupled Parents?" *Journal of GLBT Family Studies* 5 (4): 312–39.

Fisher, E.S., & K.S. Kennedy. 2012. *Responsive School Practices to Support Lesbian, Gay, Bisexual, Transgender, and Questioning Students and Families*. New York: Routledge.

Goldberg, A.E., & J.Z. Smith. 2017. "Parent–School Relationships and Young Adopted Children's Psychological Adjustment in Lesbian-, Gay-, and Heterosexual-Parent Families." *Early Childhood Research Quarterly* 40 (3): 174–87.

Hegde, A.V., P. Averett, C.P. White, & S. Deese. 2014. "Examining Preschool Teachers' Attitudes, Comfort, Action Orientation, and Preparation to Work with Children Reared by Gay and Lesbian Parents." *Early Child Development and Care* 184 (7): 963–76.

HRC Foundation (Human Rights Campaign Foundation). 2018. "Welcoming Schools." Accessed October 17. www.welcomingschools.org.

Jennings, T., & I.K. Macgillivray. 2011. "A Content Analysis of Lesbian, Gay, Bisexual, and Transgender Topics in Multicultural Education Textbooks." *Teaching Education* 22 (1): 39–62.

Jennings, T., & G. Sherwin. 2008. "Sexual Orientation Topics in Elementary Teacher Preparation Programs in the USA." *Teaching Education* 19 (4): 261–78.

Oakley, M., R.H. Farr, & D.G. Scherer. 2017. "Same-Sex Parent Socialization: Understanding Gay and Lesbian Parenting Practices as Cultural Socialization." *Journal of GLBT Family Studies* 13 (1): 56–75.

Tasker, F., & C.J. Patterson. 2007. "Research on Gay and Lesbian Parenting: Retrospect and Prospect." *Journal of GLBT Family Studies* 3 (2/3): 9–34.

Yoon, E., C.T. Chang, S. Kim, A. Clawson, S.E. Cleary, M. Hansen, J.P. Bruner, T.K. Chan, & A.M. Gomes. 2013. "A Meta-Analysis of Acculturation/Enculturation and Mental Health. *Journal of Counseling Psychology* 60 (1): 15–30.

About the Author

Anna Paula Peixoto da Silva, PhD, is an education faculty member at Valencia College. She has more than 20 years of experience working as a teacher, administrator, and teacher educator in diverse early childhood settings in the United States and abroad.

Developing Biliteracy with Intentional Support

Using Interactive Word Walls and Paired Learning

Iliana Alanís, Irasema Salinas-Gonzalez, and María G. Arreguín-Anderson

For the past decade, we three researchers have worked to improve the quality of dual language learning opportunities for young children. Our work has focused on examining teachers' strategies for nurturing biliteracy development in young bilingual learners from pre-K to third grade in dual language classrooms— that is, classrooms where students are learning academic concepts in two languages, with the instructional goal for students to become bilingual, biliterate, and bicultural (see Collier & Thomas 2009 for an expanded definition of dual language classrooms). Achieving this goal, which can be challenging (Gutiérrez, Zepeda, & Castro 2010), requires dual language teachers to do the following:

> Create situations in which children can develop and practice their first and second languages

> Use particular strategies to facilitate children's learning of academic concepts in two languages

> Plan for interactive learning (Alanís 2011; Arreguín-Anderson & Esquierdo 2011)

> Build on children's previous experience and linguistic backgrounds to help them acquire literacy understanding (García & García 2012; Soto Huerta 2012)

Accordingly, children's daily classroom experiences influence the development of biliteracy and impact the way they feel about themselves as learners. Enabling learners to try out ideas through collaborative activities facilitates language and literacy learning in a safe and nurturing environment (Magruder et al. 2013). Although classrooms where teachers ask children to work cooperatively on academic tasks are conducive for all learners, they are crucial for dual language learners, who need opportunities to hear and use language in meaningful settings (Alanís 2013).

We recognized the need for teachers to provide intentional support for daily oral language development as a means to foster children's biliteracy. In this article, we focus on the powerful use of partnering as children engage in the authentic activity of developing purposeful and interactive word walls in Spanish-English early childhood environments. Using examples from our classroom observations, we discuss how important interactive activities are for vocabulary development and suggest ways teachers can extend the daily use of interactive word walls in a dual language context. These activities, however, can be used in any context, regardless of language.

The Bilingual Advantage

Year after year, researchers are finding more benefits of bilingualism (Barac & Bialystok 2012; Bialystok & Feng 2011). A growing body of evidence suggests that bilinguals ranging from young children to mature adults exhibit enhancements in both executive functioning—a set of cognitive processes that includes attentional and inhibitory control skills—and cognitive flexibility, which aids problem solving and planning. These boosts in executive functioning and cognitive flexibility appear to result from the exercise the brain gets in switching from one symbolic code to another, and from the effort of constantly managing attention to the target language, which enhances and strengthens various brain networks. Recent studies indicate that these language-driven differences in brain activity related to executive functioning are present at an early age (Ferjan Ramírez et al. 2017) and persist throughout the school years (Arredondo et al. 2016) and into adulthood (Abutalebi et al. 2012; Stocco & Prat 2014). Interestingly, the accumulating effects of dual language experience have been linked to more robust cognitive abilities with increased age and to a lower rate of diagnosis of Alzheimer's disease (Craik, Bialystok, & Freedman 2010). Note, however, that some studies suggest that this line of research suffers from a publication bias (in which studies that show a relationship are more likely to

be published than those that find no relationship; see De Bruin, Treccani, & Della Sala 2015), and that further research is needed.

Research also shows that managing attention to two languages fosters children's metalinguistic skills (i.e., encourages them to think about language per se) (Barac & Bialystok 2012). Bilingual infants as young as 7 and 12 months have been shown to be more flexible learners of language patterns compared with monolingual infants (Graf Estes & Hay 2015; Kovács & Mehler 2009). In addition, 2- and 3-year-olds who are bilingual are more flexible learners of additional labels for previously known actions or objects (such as learning *tennis shoes* after learning *sneakers*), whereas children who are monolingual often find it difficult to add new labels for actions or objects that already have a name (McCabe et al. 2013).

Finally, studies show that bilingualism is beneficial from an economic standpoint. Across most sectors of the economy, businesses overwhelmingly prefer to hire multilingual employees (Porras, Ee, & Gándara 2014) and, among the millennial generation, multilingual employees earn more on average (Rumbaut 2014).

(From Ferjan Ramírez & Kuhl 2017)

The Significance of Interactive Word Walls for Vocabulary Development

Word walls provide a visual reference for students—a visual scaffold that temporarily assists learners in reading and writing (Harmon, Wood, & Kiser 2009; Henrichs & Jackson 2012). For example, children looking for the word *where* tend to distinguish it from *were* by the height of the letter *h*. Effective word walls offer support in the following ways:

> Scaffolding students' vocabulary development in their home language and second language

> Providing visual clues and references for language learners

> Supporting the teaching of high-frequency words

> Offering a space for students to display words that are important to them

> Promoting independence in reading and writing by building vocabulary

To best support children's reading and writing, the word wall should be a focal point of the classroom. Words, spelled correctly, should be placed at eye level so children have visual and physical access, thus creating interactive opportunities for children to physically touch or remove words as needed. When space is limited, teachers can post words from one lesson unit at a time, replacing familiar words with new words.

Teachers who design interactive word walls through collaborative activities provide opportunities for children to build sight word recognition, make connections, and read words with fluency (Henrichs & Jackson 2012). Effective efforts to promote children's vocabulary development share some of these common elements: a focus on rich and varied language experiences; teaching of words and word-learning strategies that build on children's ways of knowing; and the ability to foster word awareness at multiple levels (Graves, Schneider, & Ringstaff 2018). We argue that interactive word walls address these elements of vocabulary development when teachers provide authentic and interactive contexts in which children use the word walls in collaborative activities that focus on the children's background knowledge and language skills.

The Importance of Paired Activities in Dual Language Classrooms

Children learn by engaging in various activities with more knowledgeable peers and adults (Vygotsky 1978). Pairing students allows children to explore their new language in a social context. This social aspect of learning is embedded in cultural and social practices (DePalma 2010; Magruder et al. 2013). An effective strategy in a dual language classroom is the heterogeneous partnering of children based on linguistic and academic levels—that is, partnering children by mixed ability where one child is more knowledgeable than the other (Alanís 2011). We have observed teachers pair a child who is strong in English with a child who is strong in Spanish to create bilingual partners who facilitate each other's learning. Partnering children from two language backgrounds lets them serve as language models for one another and allows them to scaffold each other's learning through (1) active involvement of the learners, (2) use of language that is at a shared level of understanding, and (3) increased opportunities for verbal interaction. As a result, bilingual pairing becomes a learning tool for children, much like manipulatives, as they practice their language skills and reinforce their biliteracy development (Alanís 2013).

Developing Vocabulary and Fluency

When teachers create interactive word walls, they provide the context for children to learn from each other as they develop literacy (Coleman & Goldenburg 2009; Harmon, Wood, & Kiser 2009). As partners actively create and interact with the words on the wall, they increase their social and linguistic interactions, thereby increasing their opportunities for learning.

> Before reading aloud Peggy Parish's book, *Amelia Bedelia*, Mrs. Treviño, a second grade Spanish/English teacher, first asks bilingual pairs to identify homophones (words that have the same pronunciation but different meanings or spelling) they have discussed in a previous lesson. She then reads the book and asks students to help her identify some new homophones to add to the word wall. Later in the day, pairs create silly sentences using the homophones. Giggling, they share their sentences, incorporating homophones such as *ate/eight, I/eye, write/right*, and *sea/see*.

By having pairs interact with the words, Mrs. Treviño promoted multiple venues for children to practice and apply what they knew about words in fun and interactive ways.

Teachers who use paired strategies allow children to expand learning while using all their language skills (Arreguín-Anderson & Esquierdo 2011). Children can practice new and familiar words each day by looking at them, saying them, clapping the syllables, snapping the letters, and writing the words. In addition, strategies like Turn and Talk engage children in short five-minute activities in which they listen to and speak with a partner.

Ms. Oliva, a dual language kindergarten teacher, uses the Turn and Talk strategy while children are lining up for lunch: "Find two-syllable words on the English word wall and read them to your partner." Children turn and talk to the child behind them as they identify and read two-syllable words: *Henry, pizza, hello,* and *carpet.* Once everyone has had an opportunity to read a few words with a partner, Ms. Oliva asks a few of the children to share their words as she walks them to the cafeteria.

Ms. Oliva's activity helps struggling readers who may not be good visual learners and provides practice so that her students will eventually read and spell words independently.

Mrs. Rivera, also a dual language kindergarten teacher, asks her bilingual pairs to identify words from the Spanish word wall that have the same initial syllable. The children find words like *camión* (truck) and *cazuela* (pan) and write them in their spiral notebooks. Mrs. Rivera places retired words from the word walls in plastic baggies or fastens them together with a ring. She then integrates the retired words into various centers for children to review or use to play games.

(See "Word Games" for some suggestions.)

Shared Writing and Reading

When teachers discuss and use words in context, they enhance children's comprehension and retention of word meanings (Yates, Cuthrell, & Rose 2011).

Mr. Benavides, a kindergarten Spanish/English teacher, uses Morning Message as a time to model referencing the word wall as he sounds out words during a writing activity: "'It is cold and icy today. Braydon wore his jacket.' Hmm, *jacket*—does that start with a *g* or a *j*? I'd better check." He pauses to find the word he "cannot spell" on the word wall. "It's not a *g*, it's a *j*." He writes the word on the chart paper.

Mr. Benavides's modeling increases the likelihood that the children will use the strategy when they are writing and come across a word they cannot spell. It also helps children see the significance of the words located throughout their room.

Powerful instruction with word walls can also occur during conversations about books as children read and write with their peers. Read-alouds, for example, provide time to discuss and learn new words in an authentic context. As teachers read books and involve children in partner talk, children acquire new vocabulary words through meaningful communication.

During a Spanish read-aloud of *Froggy Goes to the Doctor,* by Jonathan London, Ms. Carvejal, the kindergarten teacher, pauses to discuss the word *virus* (virus, a Spanish/

Word Games

The following games reinforce word meanings through interactive activities:

> **Wordo:** Similar to Bingo, but instead of numbers, children look for word wall words in the game squares of the Wordo card (Jasmine & Schiesl 2009).

> **Word Sorts:** Children sort a collection of words taken from the word wall into two or more categories, such as nouns and adjectives.

> **Word Maps:** Children write important information about a word to make connections between the word and what they are reading or studying. Three kinds of information are included: a category for the word, examples, and characteristics. For example, a teacher pulls the word *scurried* from her read-aloud and asks students in groups of four to use their prior knowledge to guess the word's meaning. The children divide a piece of paper into four squares and write a definition, a synonym, and a sentence, and draw a picture.

> **Word Chains:** Children choose a word from the word wall and then identify three or four words to sequence before or after the selected word to make a chain. Pairs come up with words that begin with the letter that's at the end of the previous word. A category of words is usually chosen and there is a time limit. For example, after reading *Too Many Tamales,* by Gary Soto, one pair of children chose the word *tamales* and created this word chain: *tamales, salsa, apron.*

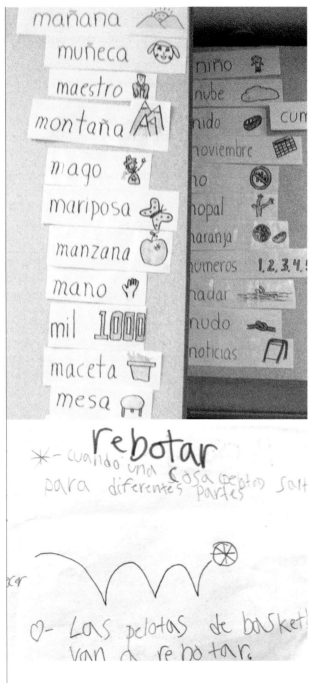

English cognate). "Habla con tu pareja. ¿Qué quiere decir la palabra *virus*?" (Turn to your partner and explain what you think the word *virus* means.) Ms. Carvejal rereads the section of the Spanish text for context. Children discuss their answers with their partners, and then Ms. Carvejal asks a few of them to share their responses. The children are unsure but know it has something to do with being sick. During the partner discussion, Ms. Carvejal writes the Spanish word *virus* on an index card to place on the word wall at a later time.

Ms. Carvejal provided opportunities for the children to use the word in meaningful sentences and to listen to the word used by their classmates—an important activity to develop listening and language skills.

On another occasion, Ms. Carvejal engages in an English read-aloud with the book *Good Boy, Fergus!* by David Shanahan, asking children to discuss with their partners the question, "How do we know Fergus was a naughty dog?" Children turn to each other and begin to retell some of the parts of the story, such as, "He broke the plant" and "He was chasing the cat." The word *naughty* becomes a word for the word wall.

Effective instruction for bilingual learners requires extensive use of realia (i.e., real-life objects or artifacts), pictures, and drawings that support children's understanding of concepts (Soto Huerta 2012).

Ms. Salinas, a second grade dual language teacher, asks partners to draw pictures to help convey Spanish word meanings. She then has partners share their drawings in small groups of four to help children practice their oral Spanish skills.

The drawings and interactions are extremely beneficial for English-dominant children who are learning from Spanish-speaking models. The additional visual and peer support provided by interacting with the word wall develops depth in their acquisition of the new language and moves them to a higher level of language ability (Alanís 2011).

Conclusion

Both interactive word walls and bilingual pairing are instructional strategies designed to facilitate language development. By creating situations for dual language learners to (1) extend their home language development, (2) use strategies to facilitate the acquisition of their second language, and (3) engage in interactive activities with peers, you can strategically help children develop oral language abilities. This planning involves focusing on what children need to learn and how to effectively teach them. When children play and work with a peer, they refine key concepts, apply new knowledge, and integrate speaking and listening in a relaxed and enjoyable environment (Alanís 2013). Building and using interactive words walls through bilingual pairing provides opportunities for sharing ideas, learning how others use reading and writing strategies, and practicing oral language skills in nurturing environments where children can rely on each other for their biliteracy development.

Reflection Questions

1. What meaningful language experiences could you create to establish a context for the use of a word wall in your classroom?

2. Besides word walls, what other resources or strategies do you (or might you) incorporate in your classroom to promote the development and practice of first and second languages?

3. Reflect on a lesson you recently taught or planned. Identify two ways you could incorporate partner-based interactions to support acquisition of academic vocabulary.

4. What are some benefits of heterogeneous partnering of children based on their linguistic and academic skills?

5. Think about a science or mathematics activity that you implemented with young children. How could you incorporate the use of an interactive word wall to promote acquisition of academic vocabulary and high-frequency words?

References

Abutalebi, J., P.A. Della Rosa, D.W. Green, M. Hernandez, P. Scifo, R. Keim, S.F. Cappa, & A. Costa. 2012. "Bilingualism Tunes the Anterior Cingulate Cortex for Conflict Monitoring." *Cerebral Cortex* 22 (9): 2076–86.

Alanís, I. 2011. "Learning From Each Other: Examining the Use of Bilingual Pairs in Dual Language Classrooms." *Dimensions of Early Childhood* 39 (1): 21–28.

Alanís, I. 2013. "Where's Your Partner? Pairing Bilingual Learners in Preschool and Primary Grade Dual Language Classrooms." *Young Children* 68 (1): 42–46.

Arredondo, M.M., X.S. Hu, T. Satterfield, & I. Kovelman. 2016. "Bilingualism Alters Children's Frontal Lobe Functioning for Attentional Control." *Developmental Science* 20 (3). doi:10.1111/desc.12377.

Arreguín-Anderson, M.G., & J.J. Esquierdo. 2011. "Overcoming Difficulties: Bilingual Second-Grade Students Do Scientific Inquiry in Pairs During a Lesson on Leaves." *Science and Children* 48 (7): 68–71.

Barac, R., & E. Bialystok. 2012. "Bilingual Effects on Cognitive and Linguistic Development: Role of Language, Cultural Background, and Education." *Child Development* 83 (2): 413–22.

Bialystok, E., & X. Feng. 2011. "Language Proficiency and Its Implications for Monolingual and Bilingual Children." Chap. 5 in *Language and Literacy Development in Bilingual Settings,* eds. A.Y. Durgunoglu & C. Goldenberg, 121–38. New York: Guilford.

Coleman, R., & C. Goldenburg. 2009. "What Does Research Say About Effective Practices for English Learners? Introduction and Part 1: Oral Language Proficiency." *Kappa Delta Pi Record* 46 (1): 10–16.

Collier, V., & W. Thomas. 2009. *Educating English Learners for a Transformed World.* Albuquerque: Dual Language Education of New Mexico, Fuente Press.

Craik, F.I.M., E. Bialystok, & M. Freedman. 2010. "Delaying the Onset of Alzheimer Disease: Bilingualism as a Form of Cognitive Reserve." *Neurology* 75 (19): 1726–29.

De Bruin, A., B. Treccani, & S. Della Sala. 2015. "Cognitive Advantage in Bilingualism: An Example of Publication Bias?" *Psychological Science* 26 (1): 99–107.

DePalma, R. 2010. *Language Use in the Two-Way Classroom: Lessons From a Spanish-English Bilingual Kindergarten.* Bristol, England: Multilingual Matters.

Ferjan Ramírez, N., & P. Kuhl. 2017. "The Brain Science of Bilingualism." *Young Children* 72 (2): 38–44.

Ferjan Ramírez, N., R.R. Ramírez, M. Clarke, S. Taulu, & P.K. Kuhl. 2017. "Speech Discrimination in 11-Month-Old Bilingual and Monolingual Infants: A Magnetoencephalography Study." *Developmental Science* 20 (1). doi:10.1111/desc.12427.

García, E.E., & E.H. García. 2012. *Understanding the Language Development and Early Education of Hispanic Children.* New York: Teachers College Press.

Graf Estes, K., & J.F. Hay. 2015. "Flexibility in Bilingual Infants' Word Learning." *Child Development* 86 (5): 1371–85.

Graves, M., S. Schneider, & C. Ringstaff. 2018. "Empowering Students with Word-Learning Strategies: Teach a Child to Fish." *Reading Teacher* 71 (5): 533–43.

Gutiérrez, K., M. Zepeda, & D.C. Castro. 2010. "Advancing Early Literacy Learning for All Children: Implications of the NELP Report for Dual-Language Learners." *Educational Researcher* 39 (4): 334–39.

Harmon, J.M., K.D. Wood, & K. Kiser. 2009. "Promoting Vocabulary Learning With the Interactive Word Wall." *Middle School Journal* 40 (3): 58–63.

Henrichs, E.L., & J.K. Jackson. 2012. "A Winning Combination." *Science and Children* 50 (3): 52–57.

Jasmine, J., & P. Schiesl. 2009. "The Effects of Word Walls and Word Wall Activities on the Reading Fluency of First Grade Students." *Reading Horizons* 49 (4): 301–14.

Kovács, A.M., & J. Mehler. 2009. "Flexible Learning of Multiple Speech Structures in Bilingual Infants." *Science* 325 (5940): 611–12.

Magruder, E.S., W.W. Hayslip, L.M. Espinosa, & C. Matera. 2013. "Many Languages, One Teacher: Supporting Language and Literacy Development for Preschool Dual Language Learners." *Young Children* 68 (1): 8–15.

McCabe, A., C.S. Tamis-LeMonda, M.H. Bornstein, C.B. Cates, R. Golinkoff, A.W. Guerra, K. Hirsh-Pasek, E. Hoff, Y. Kuchirko, G. Melzi, A. Mendelsohn, M. Páez, & L. Song. 2013. "Multilingual Children: Beyond Myths and Towards Best Practices." *Social Policy Report* 27 (4): 1–37.

Porras, D.A., J. Ee, & P. Gándara. 2014. "Employer Preferences: Do Bilingual Applicants and Employees Experience an Advantage?" Chap. 10 in *The Bilingual Advantage: Language, Literacy, and the US Labor Market,* eds. R.M. Callahan & P.C. Gándara, 234–57. Bristol, UK: Multilingual Matters.

Rumbaut, R.G. 2014. "English Plus: Exploring the Socioeconomic Benefits of Bilingualism in Southern California." Chap. 8 in *The Bilingual Advantage: Language, Literacy, and the US Labor Market,* eds. R. Callahan & P.C. Gándara, 182–205. Bristol, UK: Multilingual Matters.

Soto Huerta, M.E. 2012. "Guiding Biliteracy Development: Appropriating Cross-Linguistic and Conceptual Knowledge to Sustain Second-Language Reading Comprehension." *Bilingual Research Journal: The Journal of the National Association for Bilingual Education* 35 (2): 179–96.

Stocco, A., & C.S. Prat. 2014. "Bilingualism Trains Specific Brain Circuits Involved in Flexible Rule Selection and Application." *Brain and Language* 137: 50–61.

Vygotsky, L.S. 1978. *Mind in Society: The Development of Higher Psychological Processes.* Cambridge, MA: Harvard University Press.

Yates, P.H., K. Cuthrell, & M. Rose. 2011. "Out of the Room and Into the Hall: Making Content Word Walls Work." *Clearing House: A Journal of Educational Strategies, Issues, and Ideas* 84 (1): 31–36.

About the Authors

Iliana Alanís, PhD, is professor of interdisciplinary learning and teaching at The University of Texas at San Antonio. Her work focuses on the teaching practices in early elementary grades, with an emphasis on the effect of schooling for language minority children in bilingual programs.

Irasema Salinas-Gonzalez, EdD, is associate professor at The University of Texas Rio Grande Valley, where she teaches courses in early care and early childhood education. Irasema focuses on young dual language learners' language and literacy development through play, their development of play-based learning, and creating engaging classroom environments for them.

María G. Arreguín-Anderson is associate professor of early childhood and elementary education at The University of Texas at San Antonio. Her areas of expertise include elementary science education in dual language environments and cooperative learning in dyads.

Photographs: p. 105, © Getty Images; pp. 108, 110 (both), courtesy of the authors

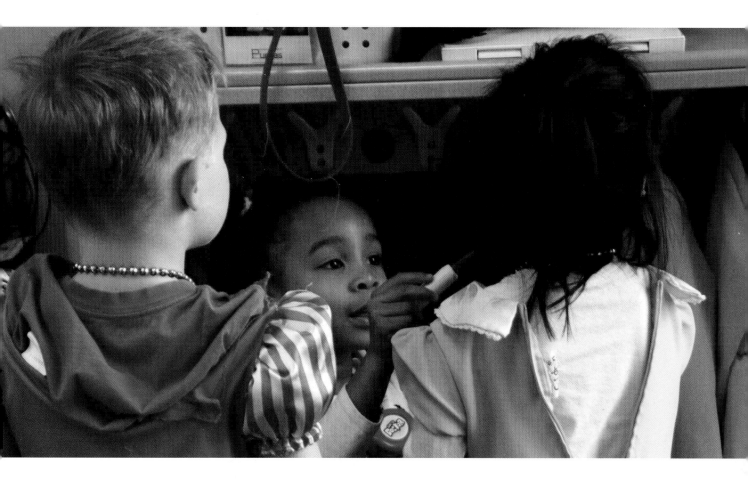

"Don't Let My Son Dress Up as a Girl!"

An Ethical Dilemma

Stephanie Feeney and Nancy K. Freeman

Four-year-old Victor enjoys playing dress-up in the dramatic play area. Typically a quiet and reserved child, he becomes a leader when playing dress-up, particularly when he is pretending to be a firefighter, princess, bumblebee, or mom. One day his father, Leo, who rarely visits the center, comes to pick up his son and sees Victor dressed in a pink princess costume. Leo is visibly annoyed and tells Meredith, Victor's teacher, that he does not want her to allow Victor to play in the dress-up area in the future. He then orders Victor to change and quickly leaves with him.

Meredith is unsure what to do. The center is devoted to fostering relationships with all of its families, and she has recently made great strides in attracting Victor's family to potlucks and school workdays. She is hesitant to take an action that might jeopardize her fledgling partnership with them. Yet she can see clearly how much Victor enjoys and benefits from his dress-up play. Meredith and the other staff believe that in addition to building children's imaginations, dramatic play enhances their social and communication skills and is an integral part of the learning process that gives children opportunities to develop abstract thinking, literacy, math, and social studies skills.

I n your work as an early childhood educator, you are very likely to face situations that involve questions of morality and ethics. You may need to weigh competing obligations to children, families, colleagues, and your community and society or make a difficult or unpopular decision. The NAEYC Code of Ethical Conduct can help you identify your responsibilities and guide your decision making when you encounter predicaments that involve ethics: considerations of right and wrong, rights and responsibilities, conflicting priorities, or human welfare. These ethical issues are apt to surface as you interact with children, families, colleagues, and community members.

The scenario in the opening of this article, featured in the Focus on Ethics column in *Young Children* (Feeney & Freeman 2017), describes a situation in which the teacher must decide if she will agree to or respectfully refuse a parent's request as well as consider how her decision will impact the class as a whole. It also brings to light a parent's strongly held beliefs that need to be acknowledged and taken into account.

Determine the Nature of the Problem

To determine whether this situation involves ethics, Meredith considers whether the terms *right* and *wrong* or *fair* and *unfair* apply. She decides that ethics is involved because she must decide the right course of action when she is confronted by Victor's angry father. She realizes it is an ethical dilemma because she could justify either agreeing to abide by the father's demand or refusing to honor it.

Analyze the Ethical Dilemma

Now that Meredith has determined that the issue she faces is an ethical dilemma, she uses the following systematic, multistep process (outlined in *Ethics and the Early Childhood Educator: Using the NAEYC Code,* Third Edition) to help her decide on a defensible course of action.

1. Identify the Conflicting Responsibilities

Meredith's training and experience have taught her that dramatic play is worthwhile for children, and she has incorporated many opportunities for them to creatively express themselves in the dress-up center as well as in other areas of the classroom. Now she must balance the benefits that Victor enjoys by taking part in dramatic play with the right of his father to make decisions about Victor's upbringing. Victor delights in this form of play with his classmates, and he might find it distressing if Meredith were to single him out by excluding him from the dress-up center to honor his father's wishes.

She realizes she also has responsibilities to Victor's classmates, who benefit from his creative ideas and leadership during these play episodes, and to her director and colleagues, who feel strongly about the benefits of dramatic play and have made it a cornerstone of their center's curriculum.

2. Brainstorm Possible Resolutions

Meredith identifies several ways to resolve to this dilemma. The two obvious ones are to agree to forbid Victor from playing in the dress-up area altogether or to ignore Leo's demand and allow Victor to play in the dramatic play area, assuming that it is unlikely that his father will see him in a princess costume again.

She admits that neither of these alternatives honors her important responsibilities to Victor and his family, and the latter option would not be ethical. That leads Meredith to consider two additional alternatives. She could continue allowing Victor to play dress-up but redirect him away from "girl" clothing and toward other props, or she could continue to let Victor choose what and how he plays while Meredith works with his father to help him appreciate the benefits of pretend play.

3. Consider Ethical Finesse

This case is a particularly good candidate for ethical finesse, a strategy for responding creatively to ethical dilemmas that meets the needs of everyone involved. Meredith is hopeful that by sharing her professional knowledge about child development and the benefits of dramatic play with Victor's father, he may begin to think differently about the situation. She thinks it might help to invite Leo to spend time in the classroom to see for himself that Victor enjoys a variety of activities, and that when he does dress up, he tries a number of different roles besides princess. She could also use the school's monthly newsletter to highlight the importance of dramatic play.

Another way Meredith might finesse this issue is by making changes to the dress-up center by offering more gender-neutral choices—such as scarves and pieces of colorful fabric—to inspire non-gender-specific play.

4. Look for Guidance in the NAEYC Code

Meredith turns to the Code's Core Values, Ideals, and Principles for guidance on her responsibilities to children and the importance of nurturing positive relationships with families.

The following Core Values (NAEYC 2016) are particularly applicable to Meredith's situation:

> Base our work on knowledge of how children develop and learn

> Appreciate and support the bond between the child and family

> Respect diversity in children, families, and colleagues

These Ideals (NAEYC 2016) also help guide her thinking:

I-1.2—To base program practices upon current knowledge and research in the field of early childhood education, child development, and related disciplines, as well as on particular knowledge of each child.

I-1.3—To recognize and respect the unique qualities, abilities, and potential of each child.

I-1.5—To create and maintain safe and healthy settings that foster children's social, emotional, cognitive, and physical development and that respect their dignity and their contributions.

I-2.2—To develop relationships of mutual trust and create partnerships with the families we serve.

I-2.5—To respect the dignity and preferences of each family and to make an effort to learn about its structure, culture, language, customs, and beliefs.

I-2.6—To acknowledge families' childrearing values and their right to make decisions for their children.

I-2.8—To help family members enhance their understanding of their children . . . and support the continuing development of their skills as parents.

Meredith locates the following applicable Principles (NAEYC 2016):

P-1.1—Above all, we shall not harm children. We shall not participate in practices that are emotionally damaging, physically harmful, disrespectful, degrading, dangerous, exploitative, or intimidating to children. This principle has precedence over all others in this Code.

P-1.2—We shall care for and educate children in positive emotional and social environments that are cognitively stimulating and that support each child's culture, language, ethnicity, and family structure.

P-2.2—We shall inform families of program philosophy, policies, curriculum, assessment system, and personnel qualifications, and explain why we teach as we do—which should be in accordance with our ethical responsibilities to children.

P-2.4—We shall ensure that the family is involved in significant decisions affecting their child.

P-2.5—We shall make every effort to communicate effectively with all families in a language that they understand. We shall use community resources for translation and interpretation when we do not have sufficient resources in our own programs.

5. Decide on a Justifiable Course of Action

Meredith decides that the best resolution to this dilemma would be to use ethical finesse to help Victor's father appreciate the value of dramatic play and to assure him that this kind of play is not unusual or cause for concern.

If finesse is not effective, Meredith realizes she should involve her director—and perhaps the other teachers in the center—in helping her determine next steps. If together they determine that restricting Victor's activities in the dramatic play area would cause harm both to him and to his classmates and therefore they should refuse to honor Leo's instruction, their decision would be guided by Principle 1.1: "Above all, we shall not harm children."

If this is seen as the most justifiable course of action, it will be essential that Meredith meet with Victor's parents to discuss her decision to continue to allow Victor to dress up and act out his desired roles. Meredith will need to be prepared to accept negative reactions to this decision.

Conclusion

This case involves strong opinions about boys' play that can be culturally determined. Many childrearing values are strongly rooted in families' cultural beliefs, and sensitive teachers must carefully balance their responsibilities to children and families—a task that can be particularly challenging when working in cross-cultural settings. Be certain you are clearly communicating with a family when you are working through a sensitive issue. The Code reinforces the field's commitment to supporting the strong ties between children and their families, to respecting diversity, and to listening to and learning from families in order to support their children's learning and development.

There is growing awareness in early childhood programs today that there are many ways for children to express their gender preferences. Early childhood educators need to

Reflection Questions

1. Do you believe Meredith would be justified in refusing to honor the father's request if her attempts to finesse this dilemma are not effective? Why or why not?

2. Have you ever encountered a situation in which a member of a child's family asked you to modify classroom activities that you believed to be beneficial? Under what circumstances might you be willing to exclude one child from a classroom activity at the family's request?

3. Imagine that you must inform a child's family member or a colleague of a resolution to a dilemma that goes against that person's wishes. Think of several ways you could diplomatically communicate your decision that would help preserve your relationship.

acquaint themselves with research on the potential impact of interfering with how children choose to explore and express their gender identity. They should also identify resources that can help families and educators understand and respond to issues surrounding children whose gender expression does not conform with the sex they were assigned at birth or with their families' expectations (see, for example, Fox 2015; Solomon 2016).

Early childhood educators may also want to consider their obligations to society at large and engage in advocacy to support the developmental needs of young children who are gender nonconforming. The NAEYC Code of Ethical Conduct points out that early childhood educators have a collective responsibility "to work toward greater societal acknowledgment of children's rights and greater societal acceptance of responsibility for the well-being of all children" (NAEYC 2016, I-4.6).

References

Feeney, S., & N.K. Freeman. 2017. "'Don't Let My Son Dress Up as a Girl!'—The Response." Focus on Ethics. *Young Children* 72 (4): 90–93.

Fox, R.K. 2015. "Is He a Girl? Meeting the Needs of Children Who Are Gender Fluid." *Advances in Early Education and Day Care* 19: 161–76.

NAEYC. 2016. *Code of Ethical Conduct and Statement of Commitment.* Brochure. Rev. ed. Washington, DC: NAEYC.

Solomon, J. 2016. "Gender Identity and Expression in the Early Childhood Classroom: Influences on Development Within Sociocultural Contexts." *Voices of Practitioners: Teacher Research in Early Childhood Education* 11 (1): 61–79.

About the Authors

Stephanie Feeney, PhD, is professor emerita of education at the University of Hawaii at Manoa. She has written and lectured extensively about professionalism and ethics and has been deeply involved in developing the NAEYC Code of Ethical Conduct, revising the Code, and developing the supplements for adult educators and program administrators.

Nancy K. Freeman, PhD, is professor emerita of early childhood education at the University of South Carolina, in Columbia. She has served as president of the National Association of Early Childhood Teacher Educators and was on its board for many years. Nancy has written and lectured extensively on professional ethics and has been involved in the NAEYC Code's revisions and the development of its supplements.

Research to Practice

New Research on Helping Young Children Develop Positive Racial Identities

Ira E. Murray and Adam J. Alvarez

Through extensive research, we know that many children in urban environments—particularly children of color and children living in poverty—are disproportionately less successful in school than their White and more affluent peers (Ladson-Billings 2006; Milner 2015). Despite popular discourses that often blame the children themselves for their academic "failure," many children of color in urban cities do not have access to adequate resources to thrive in the classroom. Two recent reports—one from the University of Pittsburgh's Center for Urban Education (CUE) and the other a joint effort from its Office of Child Development (OCD), CUE, and the Supporting Early Education & Development (SEED) Lab—highlight how societal and institutional racism play a role in denying children of color the opportunities needed to thrive in school and how helping children develop positive racial identities, particularly at very young ages, can help them overcome some of the systemic obstacles to experiencing academic success.

In their report, *Disrupting the Cradle-to-Prison Pipeline*, the Center for Urban Education investigated systemic and institutional factors that often inhibit the academic success of children of color in urban environments and, in many cases, help marshal students into the criminal justice system (CUE 2015). This trajectory is referred to as the cradle-to-prison, or school-to-prison, pipeline. CUE researchers identified 10 "roots" of the pipeline that disproportionately impact children of color, including

> School funding disparities

> Application of subjective "get tough" school disciplinary practices

> Inadequately trained teachers

> Criminalized school facilities

> Unequal access to prenatal services, early childhood education, and mental health care

Research shows that these disparities often begin early in life for children of color. A recent report from the US Department of Education's Office for Civil Rights (OCR 2016) found that Black preschoolers were 3.6 times more likely to be suspended from school than their White peers.

Despite myriad institutional and systemic obstacles, many children of color in urban contexts *are* successful in school. One avenue to success is for children to develop a positive racial identity, particularly at an early age. The report from OCD, CUE, and the SEED Lab (2016) underscores evidence that shows how forming a positive racial identity promotes higher resilience, self-esteem, and self-efficacy, which in turn counters some of the negative effects of discrimination children experience in school. However, the report also found that many families, teachers, and other stakeholders feel they do not have the resources to support the development of positive racial identity in early childhood.

Based on this and other research (see Alexander 2012; Delale-O'Connor et al. 2017; Milner 2010; Tatum 2003), we offer the following questions and recommendations for all educators to consider:

> **How can I better understand the daily realities of the children I serve?**
> Take the time to learn more about the nature of the social context in which each child lives. A context-neutral mindset fails to consider the dynamic range of children's needs that could be related to a number of external factors. In order to design interest areas, routines, lessons, and other learning opportunities that are responsive and relevant for children, deepen your knowledge of the sociopolitical histories of your students' communities and the people who make up those communities.

> **How can I build on the assets that children already possess?**
> Reframe deficit perspectives and take an assets-based approach to children and their communities. While being mindful about the context, it is essential not to make assumptions about children. Intentionally explore children's experiences and interests through genuine connections with them and their families in order to access what Luis Moll and colleagues (1992) call *funds of knowledge*.

> **How can I honor, validate, and enhance children's racial identities?**
> Promote and help develop children's racial identities. To encourage children to take pride in their racial identity, you must intentionally disrupt any of your own thoughts and practices that contribute to sustaining educational disparities. Begin expanding your racial awareness by recognizing your own race and potential assumptions and implicit biases you might hold. Then, encourage conversations about race among the children.

It is important to note that these recommendations do not lessen the need for institutional and political action to address disparities that negatively shape children's experiences inside and outside of school. These suggestions do, however, highlight ways that educators can identify, work through, and overcome systemic barriers to educational success for children of color.

References

Alexander, M. 2012. *The New Jim Crow: Mass Incarceration in the Age of Colorblindness.* New York: The New Press.
CUE (University of Pittsburgh, Center for Urban Education). 2015. *Disrupting the Cradle-to-Prison Pipeline.* Pittsburgh, PA: University of Pittsburgh.
Delale-O'Connor, L.A., A.J. Alvarez, I.E. Murray, & H.R. Milner, IV. 2017. "Self-Efficacy Beliefs, Classroom Management, and the Cradle-to-Prison Pipeline." *Theory Into Practice* 56 (3): 178–186.
Ladson-Billings, G. 2006. "From the Achievement Gap to the Education Debt: Understanding Achievement in US Schools." *Educational Researcher* 35 (7): 3–12.

Milner, H.R. 2010. *Start Where You Are, but Don't Stay There: Understanding Diversity, Opportunity Gaps, and Teaching in Today's Classrooms*. Cambridge, MA: Harvard Education Press.

Milner, H.R. 2015. *Rac(e)ing to Class: Confronting Poverty and Race in Schools and Classrooms*. Cambridge, MA: Harvard Education Press.

Moll, L.C., C. Amanti, D. Neff, & N. Gonzalez. 1992. "Funds of Knowledge for Teaching: Using a Qualitative Approach to Connect Homes and Classrooms." *Theory Into Practice* 31 (2): 132–41.

OCD (University of Pittsburgh, Office of Child Development), CUE (University of Pittsburgh, Center for Urban Education), & SEED Lab (University of Pittsburgh, Supporting Early Education & Development Lab). 2016. *Positive Racial Identity Development in Early Education: Understanding PRIDE in Pittsburgh*. Report. Pittsburgh, PA: University of Pittsburgh. www.ocd.pitt.edu/Files/Publications/RaceScan-FullReport12.pdf.

OCR (US Department of Education, Office for Civil Rights). 2016. *2013–2014 Civil Rights Data Collection: A First Look*. Data report. www2.ed.gov/about/offices/list/ocr/docs/2013-14-first-look.pdf.

Tatum, B.D. 2003. *"Why Are All the Black Kids Sitting Together in the Cafeteria?"—And Other Conversations About Race*. New York: Basic Books.

About the Authors

Ira E. Murray, PhD, is president and chief executive officer of United Way of the Capital Area in Jackson, MS. His education work focuses, in part, on ensuring children in underserved communities in central Mississippi are developmentally prepared for kindergarten. Ira received a PhD in administrative and policy studies with a focus on urban education from the University of Pittsburgh.

Adam J. Alvarez, PhD, is assistant professor of urban education in the Department of Language, Literacy, and Sociocultural Education at Rowan University. His research focuses on how race and racism shape the social context of education across various settings. Adam's work aims to support all educators, especially those who work with children of color, children living in urban environments, and children who are exposed to violence and trauma.

Building a More Inclusive Sandbox

Inviting New Collaborators to Support Children, Families, and Early Learning

Titus DosRemedios

"The truth is we need all kinds of people playing together in this sandbox. People who tweet, people who protest, people who give money, people who have meetings, people who know other people. Because there aren't enough people in the sandbox to begin with."

This quote appeared in a *New York Times* profile of social justice activist Michael Skolnik, who aptly used a sandbox metaphor to describe a challenge facing the civil rights movement in the United States (Feuer 2015). The metaphor could also apply to the field of early childhood education, which currently faces a similar challenge.

The early childhood education advocacy movement has grown steadily over the past two decades, plateaued in recent years, and currently is in dire need of reinforcements. Don't get me wrong, the early childhood education and care sector has many allies, like business leaders, elected officials, and journalists. At times, it seems everyone has climbed aboard the early learning bandwagon, and the support is welcome and often applauded by the field. By "the field," I mean those professionals doing the work of supporting, educating, and caring for young children: teachers, administrators, support specialists, teacher educators, and researchers.

The field's allies are those you might expect: advocacy groups, member associations, policy think tanks, and a growing number of the K–12 establishment (superintendents, school committees, and teachers unions). But much more support is needed if we want to reach a point in our society where all children have access to high-quality early learning opportunities before they begin kindergarten.

Funding Realities

Imagine this: all families of young children (birth to age 5) in all communities have access to a range of high-quality early learning supports that are free, friendly, knowledgeable, and engaging. Families are able to use them as often as needed. This includes play groups, children's museums, libraries, and educational supports at the pediatrician's office (like access to children's books), as well as early childhood education and care programs for infants, toddlers, and preschoolers. Identification of developmental delays and disabilities or other risk factors occurs as early as possible, followed by supports and interventions for children who need them. Families raising young children don't feel isolated and alone—on the contrary, a vibrant social network connects them to each other and to early learning and health professionals in their community. When children enroll in kindergarten, they are happy, healthy, curious, and thriving. They are ready and eager to keep learning.

This picture is what some would call a "vision of success" for early childhood education and care. But we have a long way to go to achieve it. Few children, particularly those living in households with low incomes, experience early childhood this way (Friedman-Krauss, Barnett, & Nores 2016). The harsh reality is that high-quality early childhood opportunities are subject to the economic market. Affluent families buy their children access to enriching early learning programs and experiences. Some children in families with low incomes are able to obtain entry into publicly funded programs (pending eligibility criteria, lotteries, waitlists, and budget cuts). For the remaining families, access and affordability are huge challenges—and often out of reach.

Meanwhile, "If families can't afford to pay, teachers also can't afford to stay." This well-known slogan describing the field's chronically low compensation dates back to at least the 1980s (Herzenberg, Price, & Bradley 2005; Mooney 2011) and has recently become popular again. Thanks to research by institutions like the Center for the Study of Child Care Employment (Whitebook et al. 2018), the low wages of early childhood educators have become more widely known. For example, in Massachusetts, advocates successfully raised awareness of the workforce crisis, leading to state investments in early educator salaries for five consecutive fiscal years, including $20 million in the current 2019 fiscal year budget.

This funding has helped educator salaries inch upwards, but not nearly high enough to close the pay gap with public schools: pre-K–3 public school teachers earn between $20,000 and $40,000 more per year than community-based preschool teachers (HHS & ACF 2016).

Advocates in every state are working to improve this situation and persuade elected officials to invest more resources in high-quality early education, expanding access, improving quality, and supporting the workforce. Progress has been made in recent years. Cities such as New York, Denver, San Antonio, and Washington, DC, have been expanding preschool at the local level (Muenchow & Weinberg 2016), and federal investment through competitive state grants has catalyzed significant innovation in the early learning space (Heim 2016). But continued progress is not inevitable. The National Institute for Early Education Research estimates that at the current pace of states' investment in high-quality pre-K, it would take 150 years to provide access to 75 percent of 4-year-olds (Barnett 2016). That's at the *current* pace of progress—slow and steady—here in Massachusetts. If another recession hits, or if elected officials simply focus on other issues, we could be advocating for an even longer period.

Given what research tells us about the developmental importance of the early childhood years (IOM & NRC 2015) and the numerous economic benefits generated from high-quality programming for young children (Bartik 2014), public and private investment opportunities should be apparent to most. But they aren't always obvious to—or even simply known by—the general public. So, our challenge is effectively articulating these opportunities to new audiences and allies. The field needs fresh energy, talent, and resources to help achieve its vision for young children.

Collaboration, Innovation, and Advocacy

At Strategies for Children, the policy and advocacy organization where I work in Boston, we have a unique vantage point. We have learned firsthand that it takes many different skill sets and players to effectively move state legislation and budgetary initiatives. Policy "wins" often happen when disparate actors collaborate to move an issue forward—a journalist publishes a story that gets the attention of a legislative staffer, who asks an economist for a cost-benefit calculation and shares the results with preschool advocates and coalitions that continue to press elected officials to take action. Eventually, enough policymakers know of and care about a particular issue that they make it a priority and pass a bill, increase funding, or take some other meaningful policy action. This was the case in 2005 when Strategies for Children led a broad advocacy coalition to work with the state legislature to establish the nation's first Department of Early Education and Care (Rennie Center & SFC 2008). Unlikely messengers add tremendous value to child advocacy coalitions, which is why groups like ReadyNation and Fight Crime: Invest in Kids, representing the business and law enforcement communities, are so important.

At the local community level, cross-sector collaboration is just as important. Picture a city librarian, a public housing administrator, a pediatrician, a banker, and a parent leader teaming up to expand early learning opportunities. Collaborations like these are happening in cities like Pittsfield, Holyoke, and New Bedford in Massachusetts. The citywide Pittsfield Promise coalition for reading proficiency currently includes almost 70 members from nearly every sector in the community, including banking, higher education, and health care. In Holyoke, the mayor has engaged the city police to help with an early literacy campaign. Police officers now carry English- and Spanish-language books in the trunks of their cruisers and give them out to neighborhood children (Saulmon 2013). Partners in New Bedford have established book baskets in city laundromats. Innovations like these are possible when diverse allies from various professions come together for kids. And local teams can often get partnership support from state-level organizations or national initiatives, such as the Campaign for Grade-Level Reading (www.gradelevelreading.net).

As an early childhood educator, you hold the key to as many partnerships and innovative collaborations as you can imagine. Odds are that you are already giving 110 percent to your program staff, children, families, and community. Well, if you have 10 percent more to give (early educators tend to be overachievers, so this shouldn't be too difficult), consider doing the following:

> **Tell your story.** Who are you and why is your work so important? Articulating your story and professional journey can be an empowering experience, and it is essential for shining a spotlight on the early childhood education and care field. Consider both online and traditional media outlets. At Strategies for Children, we help educators tell and publish their stories in our blog series "Voices from the Field" and "Leading the Way." Invite a reporter from the local newspaper to events at your program so your story can be shared with the larger community.

> **Invite people to the table.** Have you ever been at a planning meeting and thought, "It would be great if we could get X person to do Y for our program"? Consider inviting that

person to visit your program and start the relationship. Think of what skills or perspectives are currently missing in your group and who in the community could fill those gaps. Invite them to join coalitions and working groups. For example, school district budget directors can be valuable additions to preschool planning teams because they help balance "big vision" conversations with real financial constraints. Public health analysts can help early learning administrators stretch beyond their own programs to think in terms of the whole community, and they often have access to population-level data that educators do not. Get to know your new collaborators and their perspectives, needs, skills, and values.

> **Assign jobs.** Partners, allies, and volunteers may get complacent or burn out over time if they aren't engaged, challenged, and having fun. Think of approaching your allies as you would approach students—how might you differentiate the process to meet everyone's needs, including your own? If someone has a knack for data, ask her to lead a data working group. Does someone like taking pictures? Ask him to be your official event photographer. Tap into people's strengths, and delegate as much as possible—you can't, and shouldn't, do everything yourself. Others will want to help, especially once they visit your program and get to know the children and staff.

Build Your Own Sandbox

The next time you observe preschool children playing in a sandbox or at a sand table, pay close attention. Watch the amazing things they do with the sand and their tools. Watch how the dynamic changes when friends come to play. Note the cooperation, imaginative play, and early scientific thinking taking root as children explore cause and effect, size, shapes, and structures. Take in the engagement, the fun, the creativity.

Then think back to the sandbox metaphor and what the early learning sandbox of collaboration and partnerships looks like in your program and community. Start by inviting just one new person to the table. Tell him what you do for a living, and see if he has any ideas for supporting children, families, and early learning.

Imagine the possibilities.

Reflection Questions

1. Think of the early childhood programs and services in your local community, city, or county. Who are the key players and organizations? What are the important initiatives? What are some interesting projects or programs that are "under the radar"? The answers to these questions make up your local early childhood system.

2. What are your local early childhood system's shared goals for young children and their families? Are these goals articulated? Are they widely understood among all members of the system?

3. Do leaders at your program or initiative reflect the racial/ethnic/linguistic diversity of the young children and families you serve? If not, how might you recruit new allies from diverse populations and engage them in design, governance, and decision making?

4. Think about what skills are needed to achieve shared goals and who will need to be recruited to join the effort. For example, if the system lacks good data, how could you recruit an individual or organization with the skills needed to help gather and report currently available data?

5. Is the story of your program or initiative widely known throughout the community? If not, think about the following:

   a. Who needs to hear your story? Make a list of key audiences and stakeholder groups.

   b. How can you tell your story? Make another list of possible communication vehicles, including local press and earned media, social media, audio/video platforms, and good old-fashioned word of mouth.

References

Barnett, S. 2016. "Slow and (Un)Steady Does Not Win the Race: What Other States Should Learn From New York." *Preschool Matters . . . Today!* (blog). National Institute for Early Education Research. https://nieer .wordpress.com/2016/05/12/slow-and-unsteady-does-not-win-the-race-what-other-states-should-learn -from-new-york.

Bartik, T.J. 2014. *From Preschool to Prosperity: The Economic Payoff to Early Childhood Education.* Kalamazoo, MI: Upjohn Institute Press.

Feuer, A. 2015. "Michael Skolnik Taps His Social Network to Fight for Civil Rights." *New York Times,* November 20. www.nytimes.com/2015/11/22/nyregion/michael-skolnik-political-director-for-russell -simmons-fights-for-civil-rights.html.

Friedman-Krauss, A., W.S. Barnett, & M. Nores. 2016. *How Much Can High-Quality Universal Pre-K Reduce Achievement Gaps?* Report. Washington, DC: Center for American Progress. http://nieer.org/wp-content /uploads/2017/01/NIEER-AchievementGaps-report.pdf.

Heim, J. 2016. "Early Childhood Education Gets Push from $1 Billion Federal Investment." *Washington Post,* August 1. www.washingtonpost.com/local/education/early-childhood-education-gets-push-from-1 -billion-federal-investment/2016/07/31/a288d948-55bb-11e6-b7de-dfe509430c39_story.html?utm _term=.6172c229b21d.

Herzenberg, S., M. Price, & D. Bradley. 2005. *Losing Ground in Early Childhood Education: Declining Workforce Qualifications in an Expanding Industry, 1979–2004.* Report. Washington, DC: Economic Policy Institute. www.epi.org/publication/study_ece_summary.

HHS (US Department of Health and Human Services) & ACF (Administration for Children and Families). 2016. "Massachusetts: Access to High Quality Early Learning Matters!" www.acf.hhs.gov/sites/default/files/occ /massachusetts_wage_profile.pdf.

IOM (Institute of Medicine) & NRC (National Research Council). 2015. *Transforming the Workforce for Children Birth Through Age 8: A Unifying Foundation.* Report. Washington, DC: National Academies Press.

Mooney, C.G. 2011. *Swinging Pendulums: Cautionary Tales for Early Childhood Education.* St. Paul, MN: Redleaf.

Muenchow, S., & E. Weinberg. 2016. "Ten Questions Local Policymakers Should Ask About Expanding Access to Preschool." *American Institutes for Research Policy Center,* May 26. Washington, DC: American Institutes for Research. www.air.org/resource/ten-questions-local-policymakers-should-ask-about -expanding-access-preschool.

Rennie Center (Rennie Center for Education Research and Policy) & SFC (Strategies for Children). 2008. *A Case Study of the Massachusetts Department of Early Education and Care.* Report. Boston: Rennie Center; Boston: SFC. www.strategiesforchildren.org/doc_research/08_Rennie_Case.pdf.

Saulmon, G. 2013. "Holyoke to Promote Child Literacy by Creating 'Mini-Libraries' at Police Substations, Stocking Cruisers with Books." *MassLive,* April 25. www.masslive.com/news/index.ssf/2013/04/holyoke _to_create_mini-librari.html.

Whitebook, M., C. McLean, L.J.E. Austin, & B. Edwards. 2018. *Early Childhood Workforce Index 2018.* Report. Berkeley, CA: Center for the Study of Child Care Employment, University of California, Berkeley. http:// cscce.berkeley.edu/files/2018/06/Early-Childhood-Workforce-Index-2018.pdf.

About the Author

Titus DosRemedios, MA, is director of research and policy at Strategies for Children, an early education policy and advocacy organization based in Boston, Massachusetts. He analyzes state funding, manages strategic communications, and supports local early learning collaborations.

Discover, Learn, Grow!

Covering a broad range of subjects, this bestselling series includes articles carefully curated from NAEYC's award-winning *Young Children* journal.

Each book includes research-based articles and questions to help readers reflect on the content of the articles and on their practice. Perfect for higher education courses and in-service workshops!

NAEYC.org/shop

Spotlight on Young Children: Observation and Assessment

Item 2842
2018 • 112 pages

Spotlight on Young Children: Social and Emotional Development

Item 2850
2017 • 116 pages

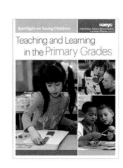

Spotlight on Young Children: Teaching and Learning in the Primary Grades

Item 2841
2016 • 136 pages

Spotlight on Young Children: Exploring Play

Item 2840
2015 • 136 pages

Spotlight on Young Children: Supporting Dual Language Learners

Item 2210
2014 • 104 pages

Spotlight on Young Children: Exploring Language and Literacy

Item 2830
2014 • 112 pages

Spotlight on Young Children: Exploring Science

Item 373
2013 • 80 pages

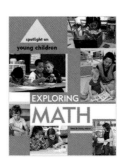

Spotlight on Young Children: Exploring Math

Item 367
2012 • 64 pages

Spotlight on Young Children and Technology

Item 267
2012 • 72 pages

Discover NAEYC!

The National Association for the Education of Young Children (NAEYC) promotes high-quality early learning for all young children, birth through age 8, by connecting early childhood practice, policy, and research. We advance a diverse, dynamic early childhood profession and support all who care for, educate, and work on behalf of young children.

NAEYC members have access to award-winning publications, professional development, networking opportunities, professional liability insurance, and an array of members-only discounts.

Accreditation—NAEYC.org/accreditation

Across the country, **NAEYC Accreditation of Early Learning Programs** and **NAEYC Accreditation of Early Childhood Higher Education Programs** set the industry standards for quality in early childhood education. These systems use research-based standards to recognize excellence in the field of early childhood education.

Advocacy and Public Policy—NAEYC.org/policy

NAEYC is a leader in promoting and advocating for policies at the local, state, and federal levels that expand opportunities for all children to have equitable access to high-quality early learning. NAEYC is also dedicated to promoting policies that value early childhood educators and support their excellence.

Global Engagement—NAEYC.org/global

NAEYC's Global Engagement department works with governments and other large-scale systems to create guidelines to support early learning, as well as early childhood professionals throughout the world.

Professional Learning—NAEYC.org/ecp

NAEYC provides face-to-face training, technology-based learning, and Accreditation workshops—all leading to improvements in the knowledge, skills, and practices of early childhood professionals.

Publications and Resources—NAEYC.org/publications

NAEYC publishes some of the most valued resources for early childhood professionals, including award-winning books, *Teaching Young Children* magazine, and *Young Children*, the association's peer-reviewed journal. NAEYC publications focus on developmentally appropriate practice and enable members to stay up to date on current research and emerging trends, with information they can apply directly to their classroom practice.

Signature Events—NAEYC.org/events

NAEYC hosts three of the most important and well-attended annual events for educators, students, administrators, and advocates in the early learning community.

NAEYC's Annual Conference is the world's largest gathering of early childhood professionals.

NAEYC's Professional Learning Institute is the premier professional development conference for early childhood trainers, faculty members, researchers, systems administrators, and other professionals.

The **NAEYC Public Policy Forum** provides members with resources, training, and networking opportunities to build advocacy skills and relationships with policymakers on Capitol Hill.

Membership Options/Benefits

NAEYC.org/membership

NAEYC offers four membership categories*—Entry Level, Standard, Premium, and Family—each with a unique set of benefits.

	ENTRY $30	STANDARD $69	PREMIUM $150	FAMILY $35
Digital articles from *YC* & *TYC*	●	●	●	●
Online networking	●	●	●	●
Local Affiliate membership	●	●	●	●
NAEYC Store discounts	●	●	●	●
Discount insurance and subscriptions	●	●	●	●
NAEYC event discounts	○	●	●	○
Retail discounts	○	●	●	○
Complimentary NAEYC books	○	◐ 1 book	● 5 books	○
Print subscription to *YC* or *TYC*	○	◐ Either	● Both	○
Online courses	○	◐ 1 course	● 2 courses	○
Access to VIP events	○	○	●	○
Access to *YC* digital archive	○	○	●	○

*Prices and benefits are subject to change. Check NAEYC.org for the most current information.

Serious Fun
How Guided Play Extends Children's Learning

Learn how to build children's knowledge through guided play, and plan learning experiences that are seriously fun!

When teachers take an active, intentional role in children's play, they greatly enrich a child's learning experience. Discover the importance of integrating rich content-based, teacher-guided instruction with meaningful child-centered play to nurture children's emerging capabilities and skills. Grow children's knowledge in areas such as math, literacy, drama, art, STEM, and outdoor learning.

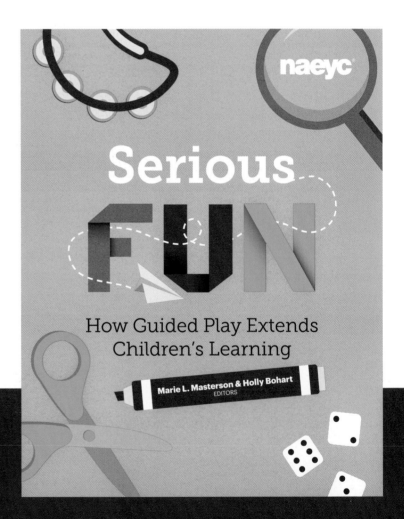

Serious FUN

How Guided Play Extends Children's Learning

Marie L. Masterson & Holly Bohart
EDITORS

National Association for the Education of Young Children